Entrepreneur First Class

(Old Truths & New Insights on Starting Your Business)

WILLIAM ANWANA

INTRODUCTION
PEOPLE, GET READY

"By failing to prepare, you are preparing to fail." – Benjamin Franklin

Dear Entrepreneur,

I salute you. I really do.

You've taken a leap of faith and decided to embark on an exciting journey: a voyage of vision, discovery and innovation, a quest to create new and wonderful things. You (and perhaps a friend or two) have spent time thinking through a problem and identifying a void - a need - that you can fill. You share the rarefied mindset of Larry Page and Sergey Brin, Bill Gates and Steve Jobs, Mark Zuckerberg and Jeff Bezos, Jack Ma and Elon Musk; people who started out with dreams and ended up living them (some still pushing the boundaries of what is possible). You have talent and skill. You've got the drive and the attitude. You're all fired up and ready to go!

But (and this is a big But) before you go out there to conquer the world, you must ensure that you are **ready**. When I say ready, I'm not referring to the state of your physical resources. The leap of faith you took, after all, most likely involved you setting out with less than 100% of your requirements. No, by 'ready', I am referring to the preparedness of your mind...of your spirit.

I know your desire to make things happen (and get paid☺) is just about ready to burst at the seams...but this is not a journey for the ill prepared. To complete it and see it through to the very end, to bring into reality the vision you can see in your mind, you will need more than excitement....

Having a great idea ready to deploy is a given; but what will make you win comprise qualities that are not seen on the surface. What distinguishes a champion fighter from the rest of the pack? Asides talent, he needs to have enhanced levels of courage, capacity, and resilience, more than his competitors. Well, you need the very same things: courage to constantly face the unknown and continually forge new paths, the capacity to deliver and stay not just in the game but on top of it, and the resilience to bounce back from failure. But most of all...you're going to need **Knowledge**.

And that, my friend, is where I come in.

You're probably familiar with the Creation Story depicted in the Bible. 'Let there be Light', God said, and there was. But wait...dig a little deeper into that passage. You may probably be taken aback to discover that 'Let there be Light' came **earlier** than the creation of the Sun,

Moon and Stars. In other words, when He said 'Light', God was **not** referring to the radiance of the solar or lunar systems which give physical light to the earth. In the original text (Hebrew) the word 'Light' (ohr) means to illuminate or to enlighten. It means...Knowledge! You need Knowledge, Wisdom, Insight.

You need to become knowledgeable in every part of your business. Every. Single. Part. You need to absorb knowledge at an increased pace and be very nimble in your thinking. You need to deeply understand why you're doing what you do. You need to develop a capacity for finance; understand and appreciate how numbers work - they have stories to tell. You need to learn how to craft a winning, well-executed business plan; and how to structure your business.

You need Light.

None of this is a walk in the park, but nothing worth having ever came easy. You've taken the most important first step and made the choice to be - and do - something different.

The next step is what you need to make your stand and own your space. And that step is **Preparation.**

As we stand at the dawn of a new world, a post-covid world, life as we knew it will no longer be the same. A new normal is emerging and we must all either adapt very quickly...or fail. The world will need a whole new set of leaders...and the leaders in this new world will be the nonconformists, the idea generators, the disruptors.

It will be you, the Entrepreneur...but only if you are ready.

This book was written just for you, to help you adequately prepare for this journey...and to shine some light on your way. Think of it as your First Class to becoming a First-Class Entrepreneur ☺

Let's go...

CHAPTER 1
PURPOSE: WHAT IS YOUR WHY?

"Every product and service is sold on the promise of a better future. The purpose of business is to deliver on the promise, and profit is the reward for doing so" – *Patrick Dixon*

First things first: let's talk about why you're doing this at all.

Before launching that idea, and taking the world by storm, take some time to first understand **why.** What is your motive for taking the road less traveled, this path of the Entrepreneur? Why were you not content to stay on in salaried employment (or not to even go into it)? In answering these questions, you will need quite a bit of reflection. And believe me you ought to reflect: this is your future at stake here. Yes, as an Entrepreneur you thrive on action, you take an idea and run with it. But certain decisions require introspection. Imagine that you're standing on the edge of a waterfall. Do you jump or not? What informs the eventual decision you make? This isn't recreational activity; it is life or death. So, if you must live (or die) for something, then you need to know 'why'!

Why is the question of the purpose for your business so critical to ask, and to answer? I think Dr. Myles Munroe captured the importance of this when he said, "when the purpose of a thing is not known, abuse is inevitable". This is a serious matter, deserving of your attention. You don't want to end up misusing resources, abusing opportunities, and wasting your time. If you have determined your destiny as that of an Entrepreneur, you must be able to clearly answer from the onset why this is so.

What is Purpose? A quick check of the word will give you several definitions, all of which will be correct to varying degrees. But let's approach it from a different angle: when you first had this great idea of yours, something happened in your mind. Sudd6enly, you could 'see' something playing out, and coming to pass. That something you saw is called a **vision.** You envisioned an idea and could see it in your mind's eye, as real as the 4 walls (or wherever you were at the time) around you.

But vision doesn't simply spring from the ether; there is a **reason** why vision exists, an objective that drives it. That reason or objective is **Purpose**; it is the 'why' of your vision. Vision is the child of Purpose; Vision flows from Purpose. You are the creator of your business, the owner of your idea, and the mother of your baby! So, before you birth that child, it is on you to fully understand what you intend to achieve through it.

Secondly, understanding the purpose behind your business helps you set the **right** priorities. Yes, there is money to be made, and hopefully your product or service will strike the right chord and your brand will become known in the market, locally or globally. But these should not be the reasons for establishing a business. Here's something to ponder on:

"If we want to know what a business is, we have to start with its purpose. And the purpose must lie outside the business itself. In fact, it must lie in society, since a business enterprise is an organ of society" - Peter Drucker.

Just in case you were wondering, Drucker is widely acknowledged as 'the father of modern management' and is one of the best-known and significantly influential thinkers on the subject of management theory and practice. He invented the concept of Management by Objectives (MBO), a strategic management model which focuses on improving organizational performance – this in turn was the precursor to Objectives & Key Results (OKRs), a framework used globally in top businesses for defining and tracking objectives and their outcomes - so it's safe to assume he knew what he was talking about☺.

What *was* he talking about though? What did he mean by that quote? Well what he was saying in effect, is that determining the purpose of business as your starting point helps you focus on the most important outcome: creating value for your intended customer. Focusing on your customer (rather than on your expectation of an overflowing back account) enables you prioritize effectively and diligently work on your idea, driven by a desire to positively impact your community, your world.

In my book 'The Antiquity of Greatness', (go get it ☺) I talk about the true meaning of greatness, which is to **serve.** Service in this sense, does not mean that you walk around subserviently, being a doormat or slave. It means to serve your **gift.** If you must be a slave, become a slave to your gift. Your business ideas are gifts to the world because they are meant to provide service to **people**; money and prominence are by-products or natural outcomes of this effect. How? Because by being customer-centric and focusing on the needs of people and the problems you can solve for them, your solutions will naturally be **valuable** to your customer base. When you are a person of value or provide a product or service of value **you get rewarded for it.** "When you make people valuable, they will make you valuable" is another spot-on quote by Dr. Munroe (you can probably tell he's an inspiration☺). In other words, making money is inevitable when you focus on serving others with your gift. This isn't rocket science; it's a Principle. And if there's anything you ought to never forget, it is this: the world runs on principles.

Let's take the idea of purposeful service a little deeper and examine its root. Do you know what you are doing when you choose to serve people through your gift? You are showing **Love;** and Love, my friend, is the greatest single power on earth. Just in case your eyebrows are beginning to raise in skepticism, think of it this way: what does it mean to love another person or group of people? When you say you love your spouse, child, parent, friend, or followers, what do you really mean? How do you show that you love them? You prove it by investing in them: sharing your time and thoughts, your gifts, and resources with them, right? Well another way to describe these activities would be as acts of **service**. And how do the recipients respond for the most part? They recognize that you love them, they open up to you, and your relationship with them deepens right? Well then, these are rewards in **response** to your acts of service. Simply put: Love begets Love.

This is what it really means to prioritize your customers and to put people first. It is a form of Love, and when people know and trust that you really care about them and value them, they instinctively respond in kind. Guess what? This is another Principle.

Generating profit is certainly a laudable objective; there's nothing wrong with this in itself. The problem arises when we make this the main purpose of our business. When we do this, we place the focus ultimately on ourselves; what **we** get out of it. This is the antithesis of service, which demands that we focus on others. I think people, consciously or not, know when you are not prioritizing them or taking time to understand their needs. And what's the result? You end up focusing less on increasing the value of your product/service and consequently the quality of your offering is substandard. Possibly you think that price slashes will cut you some slack, but don't be deceived folks: Quality trumps Inferiority every time. You can't expect continuous loyalty from customers when you don't prioritize their needs. It's like that line from *Show me the meaning of being Lonely,* sung by The Backstreet Boys: 'how can it be you're asking me to feel the things you never show?'

Hmm.

Take a while to really think about the purpose for your business. If you need further convincing of its importance, think about all the great leaders in the history of business; or at least the preeminent ones of the last 30 years. Think about the success of the businesses they built and then look at the story **behind** the success. Look at their origins.

Perhaps you admire Bill Gates, the man who gave the world the Microsoft Corporation. While you may be bowled over by his mind-blogging wealth, (with a net worth currently estimated at about $100b, I wouldn't blame you☺) it may shock you to know Gates did not found his company with this end in mind. Take a look at the vision statement of Microsoft: "a computer on every desk and in every home".

Still need more convincing?

How about the vision statement of Amazon, brainchild of the (currently) richest man on the planet: "...to be earth's most customer-centric company; to build a place where people can come to find and discover anything they might want to buy online".

Here's that of Facebook: 'People use Facebook to stay connected with friends and family, to discover what's going on in the world, and to share and express what matters to them".

Apple: "We believe that we are on the face of the earth to make great products and that's not changing".

Google: "to provide access to the world's information in one click".

What strikes you about these vision statements? Clearly stated? Sure. Concise and to the point? Certainly. But read them again; what is the driving motive central to each one? They reflect a desire and focus to provide service of some kind...to people! It was through consistently focusing on their aspiration to live up to their visions and provide valuable services to people that these companies became what they are. Quid pro quo, if you will.

This is the key to becoming great in the entrepreneurial space: focus on continuously solving problems and providing quality service to people. Let this be the driving spirit of what you do, and you and your business will be transformed and rewarded a 100 times over.

Guaranteed.

CHAPTER 2

THE BUSINESS: REGISTRATION & STRUCTURE

"No business can succeed in any great degree without being properly organized"
– James Cash Penney

Business Structure

Once you're clear in your mind about the vision and purpose for your business, it's time to get into the nitty-gritty, and registering your business should be at the top of your list. But before we examine why this is so important, let's first have a look at the types of businesses which actually exist (in the legal sense of the word). This should further assist you in deciding what type of business structure best suits you so you can register accordingly. Our nomenclature here depends in which country you're doing business but should help you appreciate general principles.

Possibly the best way to understand the differing nature of business entities is by benchmarking them against a pivotal concept: limited liability.

Limited Liability

High-sounding? Not really. The clue is in the name itself. A liability infers that you have an obligation to pay a debt in some form or other, doesn't it? Well then, a **limited** liability means that the obligation is narrowed or restricted. In other words, your obligation would not be as much as you may have ordinarily paid, under certain circumstances.

We'll go into registration specifically in a minute but let's buttress the above assertion with an example. Assume your business is already up and running; you've taken out a loan from a bank to cater to your financing needs. A few months down the line though, the business developed some issues and you are now behind on repayments. The bank gets uncomfortable and doesn't want to support you anymore; after all you are a new customer and they already feel they took a chance on you by advancing you credit in the first place. So, they will do what banks tend to in these circumstances: demand their money back!

Because you took the loan in your name, you and you alone are responsible for paying back every last cent. And if things degenerate to the point where you are taken to court, the bank will have the right to take over any asset you own to recover the loan.

This scenario describes what is known as an "unlimited liability"; meaning that depending on how much you owe, everything you own (whether in the business or as a personal asset) will be sold until the loan amount is fully settled, or you become bankrupt!

Oops.

But let's flip the script and instead assume the business was registered as a limited liability. Well in this scenario what you must pay will be **limited** to a fixed sum (usually how much you personally invested in the business). Bottom line: with a limited liability business, you will not have to forfeit your personal assets in the event of litigation.

Hallelujah? ☺

Naturally, our hope is that you don't end up facing such circumstances, but in business the wise thing to do is prepare for every possible contingency.

Now that you understand the limited liability model you can now appreciate the various types of registered business entities. Here they are:

- **Sole Proprietorship**: is owned and operated by a single individual (hence 'sole'). The business and its owner are one and the same – in the eyes of the law. Sole Proprietorships are the simplest types of businesses to set up; it's just you, your idea, and your ability to make it work. There's little start-up capital required; you just plug and play, as it were.

A Sole Proprietorship is clearly a classic example of an unlimited liability business because you are totally responsible for all risks and rewards, not to mention the fact that business continuity is impossible if you retire, become disabled or pass on. A lot of newbie entrepreneurs run sole proprietorships; you will find this type of business works best for small traders, shop owners and artisans (plumbers, carpenters etc.) who typically work alone in their business.

- **Partnerships**: are usually owned and operated by a minimum of two partners. While partnerships do not normally enjoy limited liability, in many countries, there are Limited Liability Partnership arrangements where the liability of owners is restricted to their investment in the partnership. You'll commonly find professionals (lawyers, accountants, consultants etc.) operating partnerships.

- **Private Limited Liabilities:** are the most popular and common types of business entities. Under the law, a Limited Liability Company is invested with the rights of human being, meaning that it can own property, borrow, and lend money, sue, and be sued. Its assets and liabilities are totally separate from those of its owners; for this reason, Limited Liabilities are quite popular with entrepreneurs and businesspeople. The best part is, because this type of entity exists on its own, it can be sold or transferred to another person if the owners (shareholders) so wish. Private Limited Liability businesses are perfect for the modern entrepreneur who wants to start a business and grow it into something significant. It is suitable for all kinds of industries: from agriculture and manufacturing to IT and professional services. While it's a bit more expensive to set up than sole proprietorships and partnerships, the benefits are worth the expense.

- **Public Limited Liability Company (PLC)**: This is virtually identical to the Private Limited Liability Company; the major difference being that a PLCs is **publicly** owned, and its shares are traded on stock exchanges where anyone can buy and sell them. The costs of setting up a PLC are significantly higher than all the other types of businesses previously stated and because they deal in the public domain, the rules and regulations surrounding the governance of PLCs are quite rigorous. PLCs are perfect for very large companies that may have been in business for a while. Usually, most companies start as private limited liability companies then transit to becoming public limited liability companies.

Why Register Your Business?

In answering this, let's first deal with a common misconception you may have about business: that you can operate a successful one indefinitely without registering it.

It's not that you can't establish one: virtually anyone can start operating any kind of business whatsoever; all you need is to think up a product or service, get people to patronize you and presto – you're 'in business'. That's not the issue; the fallacy lies in thinking you can continue operating one perpetually, without having to get it legally registered. Well, technically you could, but for an entrepreneur serious about developing a business (that's you, by the way☺), registering it is not just a smart move – it's a necessity.

Really now, think about it: who owns a business that doesn't legally exist? Because that it is precisely what an unregistered business is - a non-existent one. I understand the temptation to postpone (or out rightly avoid) registering your business, particularly when you're just starting out and seem to have found a measure of success. But is that all there is to your business? Are you content to operate within a small pond, no matter how big your fish becomes?

Remember your vision and purpose. All your hard work and strategic thinking will not amount to much at the end of the day if you refuse to do something as basic as getting your business registered. Seriously, if this were the one thing holding you back from significant success, wouldn't you do it? You would. So why not just do it now? It may very well be THE thing that propels you into the higher dimension, like my wife would say - she uses that word a lot☺.

But enough preaching; let's talk about the critical reasons for business registration. By the time you're through, you wouldn't waste another minute!

- **Identity**: Say you've come up with a really cool concept and business name. But you dilly-dally about registering and continue operating; by the time you've read this book and are convicted to register, you discover another smart chap had the same idea for a name (different business) but unlike you, registered immediately. Well guess what? His business name is the one which is legally recognized; yours is not. You're now stuck with having to think up another name after operating with one for a while; not to mention the confusion you would cause your customers. Some of them may conclude that you are either unserious or engaged in some illegal business and promptly leave! Registering your business (on time) ensures that your name and concept are **legally recorded;** the first act of a Business Registration Office is ensuring no other business already exists with the same name. This is a legal requirement as no two businesses should have the same name to avoid confusing the public. Once this is confirmed, you can complete the registration process and begin using the name. One great thing about registering your business is that no other business can use or register the same name. Ever. Well...unless your business goes bankrupt and is formally dissolved...but I rebuke that on your behalf☺.

- **Personal Liability Protection**: Perhaps the single most important benefit of business registration is protection from personal liability. As we have discussed earlier, without this protection, there is a strong possibility that you could forfeit not only your business but also your personal property, in the event of litigation. If assets belonging to your business are involved in fatalities or accidents and you are sued for damages, you are liable to pay. However, where your business is registered as a limited liability entity, the worst case scenario is that the responsibility for paying damages would lie solely with the business, because it is a separate legal entity from you, the owner. But remember: only a **Limited Liability** company can provide this protection.

- **Quality of Clientele**: If you're keen about running a serious business, realize that your customers will expect it to act like a serious business. Most customers (especially corporates), expect a responsible business to be registered and will not transact with an unregistered one; in certain cases, it's actually against the law to operate an unregistered business due to regulatory and tax implications. Consider a moment: would you do business with an organization that cannot issue receipts? Well, you can't if you are not registered! You get where this is going? You cannot run a proper business without registering – unless your aim is to run an excellent petty trading business and be relegated to the streets, in which case...good luck to you. The success of your business depends a great deal on the credibility and perception of your brand. If your customers have no sense of confidence in your business, you have no business.

- **Financing**: This one is really a no-brainer: no serious lender or investor will deal with an unregistered business. Registering your business is an absolute, non-negotiable prerequisite in getting financed, whether through equity or debt (more on equity and debt financing later, for now bear in mind that these are the 2 major methods of gaining additional funding for the business). So, in either case you will not get any funding as it is highly unlikely for lenders or investors to loan money to, or invest in, an unregistered business that has no formal structure. End of story.

- **Business Continuity**: Remember back in the introduction I said you shared the same rarefied mindset as some of the best-known global entrepreneurs so many of us admire? You do. But asides mindset, there's another quality those names have in common which you also need to imbibe, and that's the attitude of business continuity. You see, the owners of these businesses set up structures which would outlive them. When these guys move on, their businesses would remain, if run properly (case in point: Bill Gates). It's the same with the global brands we know today which have their origins in earlier centuries.

Does the name John Pemberton ring a bell? Possibly not. But I bet 'Coca-Cola' does! Well, Pemberton was the gentleman who invented the original formula for this world-wide drink...in 1885. He has long since left this earth, but the Coca-Cola brand has lived on, and no doubt will continue to. How's that possible? Through Continuity: ensuring the business is trans-generational. Well guess what, business continuity is only possible if you **register** your business, irrespective of how many great ideas you may have on how it would live forever. When your business is registered, only then does it have the legal potential to become an asset that transcends generations with an unlimited lifespan. In years and decades to come, not everyone may remember your name...but they just might remember the business you left behind.

Organizational Structure

Business structure and organizational structure may sound like similar terms, but they have and fulfill different purposes.

Organizational vs. Business Structure

While Business Structure refers to the legal status and description of a company (such as sole proprietorship or limited liability) which involves tax status and legal regulations, Organizational Structure is the relationship between the different roles in an organization. It helps you identify each role and link them together, while also enabling you decide the level of responsibility each role involves or ought to have. Essentially, a proper organizational structure shows the order of roles within the organization. Developing a clear idea of what the organizational structure of your business should be at the outset, will assist in giving it a proper grounding through the start-up phase and beyond.

Business Evolution

Why the need for hierarchical structure? Well, even if you start out as a sole proprietor, after a while as you seek to grow and expand (which is only natural), you will sooner or later realize that it is impossible for you to efficiently perform all functions, especially those that require some form of managerial capability. You will then employ others to help you in the work and will give those who are dedicated, the responsibility of managing various functions according to their capabilities (such as finance, sales & marketing). In other words, you delegate important tasks you cannot accomplish on your own (at least not simultaneously). When you delegate these managerial responsibilities, you as the owner of the business, are now free to focus on larger goals, such as thinking through the development of the business, in which direction the ship should be steered: you know, business owner stuff☺. At the same time the employees trusted with the responsibilities grow increasingly skilled in performing those functions and the result is a business that is overall, more efficient.

No need to be Complex

You don't need to hire a consultant to get your structure or organizational chart developed☺. For the typical Small Business, a very simple structure will do, which you can use in the start-up phase, and which you can often continue to use long after this phase. This is because you will typically have few employees so the complex structural decisions that large corporations regularly face will not be one of your stress triggers for quite a while. Your structure at this time will most probably comprise just you (owner/manager) and a few employees in different roles underneath you. If you are working with partners, then the structure should show all the partners (including yourself naturally☺) at the top.

Developing the Chart

Developing an organizational chart is as simple as thinking through the roles and hitting the 'SmartArt' tab in the 'Insert' function of a word document...which is what I just did☺ and voila...you have a chart that looks like this:

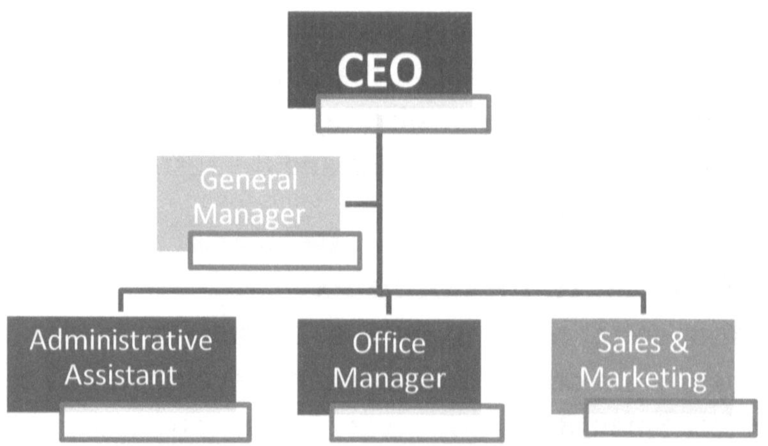

If your structure at this point is extremely simple (you and one other person, for example), it's not necessary to develop a chart. But in thinking ahead (as a good business owner should) and if your structure includes more than two levels of hierarchy (i.e. if it goes beyond owner/manager and employees), a chart can be useful. Boxes like those in the above can be used for each position (highest at the top) with the next ranking office below that and so on. You can distribute copies to all employees so everyone is officially on the same page: a who's who, as it were.

It really is that simple. However, for those who seek more 'artistry' or pizzazz with their charts, here's a cool link that may help: https://www.orgcharting.com/corporate-org-chart-templates/

No need to thank me…you've already bought this book, haven't you? ☺

CHAPTER 3
STANDARDS: ALIGNING WITH EXCELLENCE

"Excellence is never an accident. It is always the result of high intention, sincere effort, and intelligent execution; it represents the wise choice of many alternatives - choice, not chance, determines your destiny." - Aristotle

One of the more underestimated, yet key, characteristics that distinguish great companies are standards. Well-run, successful businesses responsibly hold themselves to high standards and ensure these permeate throughout the company.

Everybody wants to own or be a part of great companies, right? So how come we don't have more great organizations? I think part of the answer is that quite a few businesses (large or small) don't effectively use standards, or at the most only pay lip service to them.

Let's look back to our closing thoughts on Purpose. Essentially, we noted that great companies focus on providing quality service to people, and through consistently working on this goal, they became valuable businesses in return.

The key word here is **quality.** Odds are that yours is not the only business providing a particular product or service, so you are contending for customer share and loyalty in a competitive marketplace. Clearly, your business needs to be differentiated to stand out and you need to develop a brand that speaks to excellence, value, and class. It doesn't matter that you're just starting. From the get-go your objective should be distinction and to eventually be numbered among the greats (after all, why become an entrepreneur if you're only going to be an average or mediocre one?)

But then, how do you define quality? How do you know if the product or service you are providing can be said to be best-in-class? Because you really are in a class. Think back to your school days: back in school, tests and examinations were used to separate the intellectually gifted from the average and not-so-gifted students. A benchmark was set and defined as the average score you should rank above to qualify as a top student in the subject, or the overall class.

That is precisely how standards work in business. When you meet what is considered the agreed, defined benchmark of quality; the established norm, or requirement, your output – and business - can be said to be of **industry standard**.

Standards shouldn't be relegated to one part of the business; they should be an established culture throughout the business. There's no point having quality salespeople for instance, if your product is below industry standard. Standards should revolve around everything: the product, process, delivery system and supply – the full range of activities the business engages in which directly or indirectly, eventually impacts on the customer. Remember the correct purpose of a business is to create value - for your customer.

Perhaps you're thinking as a beginner or relative unknown, you don't have to stress about standards; just ensure you're getting product out anyway?

Wrong.

It is the practice of aligning your business to industry standards that provides the opportunity for you to stand out. You must realize that as a small business, you need to work extra hard to prove yourself against the big boys in your field. It is through ascertaining and aligning with standards that your competitive advantage lies; smaller businesses are able to move more quickly than their larger counterparts; and when they deliver service of similar (or higher) standard they can expand their customer base more rapidly and open doors to new markets.

Do not underestimate the power of word of mouth; the more customers get to know you and realize that even as a small business you're still providing product that can compete favorably with high-end companies, the more you are able to broaden your customer base (aka become more valuable).

When you implement proper standards, you inspire the confidence of customers in your business and set it apart from competition. More importantly, standards accrue benefits to your bottom line by assisting to reduce costs and boost productivity, both of which invariably improve profits. You are also likely to discover that some contracts and supply chains will only be available to businesses which are standards compliant.

Standards are proven methods of working more efficiently and effectively. They help organizations improve their performance, reduce their risk, and help them be more sustainable. Working with standards can help you to depend on every member of your staff to drive the performance of the business - no matter where they are in the organizational structure - because everyone is guided by the same core principles.

Organizational standards outline the way in which business is to be conducted and regulate what is agreed as acceptable behavior in the workplace e.g. the phone will be answered within three rings.

Generally, a company will establish and communicate standards in relation to:

- **Customer Service**: Service standards can refer to both internal and external customers. Giving a sense of how the business is perceived by its employees and clients.
- **Code of Conduct**: These define acceptable behavior in terms of interpersonal relationships; aka how do employees treat each other in the workplace.
- **Human Resources**: Human resource standards relate to issues concerning staff (compensation, allowances etc.).
- **Quality Assurance**: relates both externally (external quality accreditation such as ISO) or internally (business auditing and process reviews).
- **Staff Presentation**: how you decide your staff should dress. This could be general or specific depending on the type of business (i.e. whether a uniform is worn or not). In the general sense, it deals with how you want your staff to look as representatives of your business.
- **Corporate presentation**: the external image the business wishes to project. For example, a company may state no graffiti or posters should be seen anywhere in the building.

All these may sound very grandiose and unnecessary, but I would strongly urge you to note that if you want to build a business of excellence then you must be able to align with standards. It is important that your standards are communicated and easily accessible to both employees and customers. Customers can measure your actual output against the standards you have set; when a company is able to consistently reach a predefined measure, customer loyalty is increased.

So how do you develop effective processes, procedures, and standards for your business?

It's probably a good idea to do some research on the standards business leaders in your chosen industry are practicing. Remember that you are setting up to compete with them, and you must develop your own business to at least be at par with the output of competition. From there you should:

- **Document**: you probably want to develop a Standard Operating Procedure manual that spells out how you want to operate and the quality you seek to hold your business.
- **Ensure** the standards are based on the vision and strategy of your business.
- **Inculcate** this in your staff training program as your staff strength increases.
- **Practice** what you preach: ensure you are actively practicing the standards (your staff will be watching to follow your lead).
- **Discuss** the standards regularly in your meetings and encourage feedback (be flexible and open to improvements).

- **Regularly** review and update; business is dynamic and there are bound to be changes along the way which will impact how you conduct it.

Once you've met the demands of the standard, certification allows you to promote it, making you stand out from the crowd.

ISO Certification for Startups?

Well, why not? Startups mainly work on their survival in the increasingly competitive business world while generating revenue. For any business, building customer **trust** is essential because this is what enables you acquire those customers who will stick with you through the long haul. It is these types of customers that are critical to the success of startups and their business growth.

Obtaining ISO certification goes a long way in escalating this trust, asides the obvious benefit of optimizing processes.

While they are generally for larger companies and not mandatory for startups, it may be a good idea to include getting an ISO certification for your business in your short/mid-term plan due to several benefits, some of which are:

- **Enhanced credibility and Image**: as an ISO certified business; you have demonstrated that it follows internationally recognized standards, which of course improves your brand perception.

- **Marketing Device**: You can use it as a powerful marketing tool; it's certainly easier to promote an ISO certified product or service.
- **Quality of Clientele**: If your business is competing for public sector tenders or getting projects from large enterprises, ISO certification increases the chances of success.
- **Customer Satisfaction/Loyalty**: Quality management principles are the foundation requirements for ISO, and following these principles ensures customer satisfaction. If you didn't already know, then realize that satisfied customers = retained customers. Furthermore, loyal customers don't only make repeat purchases, they also spread the 'gospel' of your brand...which means new customers!
- **Increased Revenue**: With a smooth sales and marketing process, the business can increase revenue and market share. And really, who doesn't want an enhanced bottom line?

ISO certifications help in proving to customers that you are a well-run business which aligns with international standards. They also help to enhance the quality of your product/service and your overall business environment, which improves the trajectory of your business.

Think about it.

CHAPTER 4

YOUR BRAND: SPEAK (CORRECTLY) TO THE MARKET

"A brand is a voice and a product is a souvenir." – Lisa Gansky

'What's in a name?' queried Juliet in a famous soliloquy from William Shakespeare's *Romeo & Juliet.* 'That which we call a rose by any other name would smell just as sweet' concluded the character. In other words, what a person or thing is called is independent of its inherent quality. If the flower we call the rose was instead known as the fog leaf, it wouldn't make a difference to its essential nature; the bard was pointing out that the **content** of a thing or person superseded its **name**.

Brilliant guy wasn't he ☺.

Similarly, Dr. Martin Luther King Jr touched on the spirit of this assertion in his famous 'I have a dream' speech as he thundered 'I have a dream...that my four children will one day live in a nation where they will not be judged by the colour of their skin, but by the **content**

of their character' , the conviction of his statement propelled by the power of his voice.

Wonderful William…but…what exactly do Shakespeare and King have to do with my brand???

Ok then; remember in the Registering the Business chapter, I mentioned that the quality of your brand plays a critical role in the success of your business.

What I want you to understand, is that the power of your brand is not in its **name**: your name is only as effective as the business! In developing names for our business, I believe our hearts are in the right place and we want the aspirational objectives we have in mind for our company to reflect in what we name it (this is rather similar to how children are named in Africa; we believe that what we call our child will align with his nature). So if I had a business named, for example, Premier Consults, the impression I most likely want to create in your mind when you see or hear that name, is that it is the leading or foremost company in the field of consulting.

But here's the thing: if you decided to take me on because you believed in the promise embedded in the name of my business, but all you got was consistently poor service and output, what would you think of the business then? Certainly not premier! Your impression would be negative, and you would probably do your best to dissuade people you know from dealing with me.

That is the true impact of a brand: its quality.

Why does the quality of a brand play such an important role to its success? Here's a short list of some really great brands:

Coca-Cola.
Microsoft.
Apple.
Tesla.
Oprah.
Ali Baba.

What springs up in your mind when you hear or think about these names? How cool they sound? ☺ Probably not…rather, you think about the quality they represent.

Developing a great brand is essential to your long-term survival as a startup; but too many businesses grab the wrong end of the stick and think that developing a brand means marketing it.

I remember once listening to the radio and hearing a great ad for a fast food outfit which focused on its fried chicken product. I say the ad was great because it accomplished its objective: the voice over artist was a genius; he was so effective in communicating how succulent the chicken tasted, how it was fried to perfection, how the flesh smoothly came off the bone with one bite, how just the right sauces were used, that I actually started to salivate (call me a foodie if you want ☺) . The ad promised an optimal experience for the chicken-eating lover, so the nearest chance I got, I headed off to the outfit and ordered a large pack of fried chicken. But far from the tasty, succulent chicken the voice on the radio had promised in dulcet tones, I was offered far too oily and far too crunchy over-seasoned chunks of chicken. 'So much for coming right off the bone' I remember thinking bitterly.

What went wrong here? There was an effective marketing strategy, but the product did not live up to its promise. The result did not align with the message it had marketed as a brand. When asked by my buddies, I told them not to bother.

Marketing, my friend, is the icing. It is not the cake.

Let's first talk about where businesses tend to get it wrong from a brand perspective and then look at how you can develop a great brand:

- **Surface over Substance**: Think about an iceberg. Are you aware that only about 20% of it is what you actually see? The significant portion of the iceberg is submerged. Well, this also holds true for brands: only a relatively small part of a brand is what we (the public) see, the real content of the brand is not immediately visible, but it is what drives the business. It is the way you work, the quality of your product/service, the quality of your staff, your processes, your culture.

Too many businesses focus on the 20%, the exterior, the 'image' of the business; but while perception is important, it should not be your priority. Remember that chicken outfit I mentioned? My 'perception' of them when I heard the ad was totally positive and I was drawn to the brand because I believed in the promise of their marketing campaign. But we know what happened afterwards. I was not convinced to continuously patronize (the suave ads did not stop). This is why the main part of your work in brand development must be inwards, below the surface. As a startup you will not have had the opportunity to show a consistent performance; but what you **can** show is your personality, your vision, the meaningful idea you are bringing to the table. These are what constitute your 'brand capital' and what your reputation in the marketplace would be built on; this is how you begin to earn trust. Of course, you need a brand name that is expressive and you sure need a cool logo but these will not help you if the **core** of the brand – what it stands for -has no depth. That's the point.

- **Prioritizing brand awareness**: you want a lot of people to know about your business, I get it. More awareness = more customers = success, right? Well...wrong, actually. Think about it this way: if you are all over the place in terms of exposure but there is no clear definition of what the brand is offering and what makes it attractive, what do you think the end result will be? You should start by making it attractive to a core group of people who can identify with the brand and spread the word about it. Remember, you are in a competitive market environment and are likely not the only business doing what you do; if there are brands more attractive than yours which are also competing for the same business, your chances of survival are...slim to none! If you desire to be an effective brand, focus on creating attractiveness...not awareness.

- **Lacking clear positioning:** are you able to describe what makes your business unique and what distinguishes it from rivals? You should. You must. If you cannot, then you don't have a good idea of how you should position your brand in the market. What consumers want to know is that YOU are the best, that you are numero uno. People want quality! And if you can't clearly state how you are No. 1 or why they should see you in this light then you are in danger of losing out. You must focus on the core of the brand (that thing which makes it unique) and then make it your goal to permanently defend this position. This means that anything that does not contribute to this objective, should be discarded. You are not in business to know and do everything. But you should show that you are the best at the one thing you DO know and then do that thing better than anyone else. That's a brand!

So, what do you need to build a great brand?

Looking at the weaknesses described above, we can infer that a great brand begins with asking 3 major questions:

- What is the **core** of the brand?
- What makes it **unique**?
- What is its **focus?**

When you have truthful answers to all 3, you have a great foundation to build your brand.

The advantage that startups have over their larger counterparts is that they can begin their life on a new and fresh basis and work on consistently translating their vision into reality. Where they lack awareness and permanence, they have the benefit of agility and boldness. Where they are disadvantaged by stability and reputation, they offset this with agility and courage. They can challenge the status quo and punch above their weight; they can fall to rise again.

A strong brand is crucial for the survival of startups because it is the repository of the values and vision of its owners.

So, get to work on developing your brand; focus on delivering strong and unforgettable performances, focus on value creation and focus on communicating these effectively.

Your brand is your voice in the market: Speak!

CHAPTER 4

CREATIVITY: THE SPIRIT OF INNOVATION

"Innovation distinguishes between a leader and a follower." – Steve Jobs

Let me ask a question.

Actually, 2 questions.

First: are you aware that everything that was created in this world...is still here?

Think about it: precious stones, mineral resources, metal, wood. Name it. These have always been part of the Earth, and they weren't put there by human hands.

If you agree with this, then here's the second question. You might think it hilarious or a little silly...but try to answer anyway: why weren't the folks who lived in the first century able to build an airplane?

Every material in the exterior and interior of a plane and what propels it existed in the 1st century as much as it did when the Wright brothers appeared on the scene. So why couldn't our first century forebears build a plane?

Answer: Knowledge.

But more specifically: Innovation!

You see, anything and everything Man ever made has always been from a combination of **old** things; things that were already existing around him. The wood that chairs are made from was already in trees! The carbon filament and wires that Edison used in inventing the lightbulb were already in the earth! Everything you see around you, every man-made contrivance, was made from pre-existing materials or objects.

So, when we talk about Innovation, it has nothing to do with **new** things. But here's the secret: the difference between an innovative individual and one who is not, lies...between...their...ears.

The difference between the Wright brothers and our first century ancestors is that they had a **vision.** They then acted on that thought and combined things that were already existent, to produce a mind-blowing result. It was Edison's **vision** of an incandescent bulb that drove him to continuously work with materials that were already available to produce the lightbulb. The same materials were available to the contemporaries of Edison and the Wrights – but only these men produced what they did because they had **vision.**

The heart of innovation is vision.

Vision is not what you can see physically, but what you do see even when your eyes are closed. Ray Charles and Stevie Wonder were both struck by blindness from very early ages, but they developed the gift of music that was within them, and served it to the world, propelled by their vision!

Vision is the capacity to see beyond your eyes.

You became an Entrepreneur because you had a vision. An idea. And you want to make it a reality. But it is not enough that you have a vision...you must constantly innovate in order to remain valuable. Do you think that's possible or not?

Let me tell you why I think it is.

Some say the world is full of problems...and really, looking around us, we can readily attest to that fact. But here's the flip side of that assertion: every problem in the world is an opportunity waiting to be solved. The question is: do you see it as a problem...or as an opportunity?

A true innovator knows that there really isn't a problem...there's only an opportunity to be creative. You have to be able to see things differently; to look at 'old'' things in a new way and dare to try something that has never been tried before.

You can do this. And I say this not as a cheap attempt to 'motivate' you...but because I know something about you: you were born with a creative spirit.

Let me drive home this point in a roundabout way...
My siblings and I owned a dog once (our second...or was it our third). He was a cute little fella, a Lhasa mixed breed we called Baggio (for what reason I have absolutely no idea!). We all loved him...but I think I did most of all, as he was with me longest (my other siblings having moved out of town). I raised him from when he was a puppy and he stuck to me like glue - whoever called dogs 'man's best friend' certainly had a point ☺. I could anticipate Baggio's every need and attend to it; feeding time was one of the periods I looked forward to the most. I would grin as he jumped on the bowl of whatever doggie grub was placed in front of him and watch amusedly as he wolfed it down, jaws crunching away, tongue darting out every 10 seconds to lick around his muzzle and then he would grin at me (don't ask me how dogs grin, but he did).

One day I thought about how he ate (wolfing down, jaws cracking) was so different from the way I ate...and that I ate with plates and cutlery, but he ate from a bowl. And if I had lived 500 years ago, even if I wasn't eating with ceramic plates, it would have been with some form of cutlery, but Baggio would have eaten exactly the same way.

Here's the point: regardless of your beliefs about the origins of humanity (divine creation or natural evolution), I think we can agree on one thing: the nature and abilities of man are different from those of animals. We've both been around for millennia, but while animals have continued to eat how they've always done, Man progressed from eating out of leaves, to pods, to wooden bowls, to golden and silver plates, to ceramic ones.

We have changed and continue to change; they have not.

There is something in us that drives to evolve, to want to know more, to learn more, to do more, to be more.

That is your creative spirit, the spirit of innovation. And each and every one of us has this spirit. But just like how some seeds are planted and others are thrown away, the results of creativity (or seeming lack of it) are produced by how we treat it.

Some see sheep; others see clothes. Some see crocodiles; others see footwear.

What do you **see?** Is your creative vision 20/20?

Or do you covet the sight of others?

Bruce vs. Jackie

Quick test: who is the most popular martial artist that ever was?

If you guessed 'Bruce Lee', you were right on the money.

Lee is the most iconic Asian-American film star, probably as recognizable by his signature fight moves as Michael Jackson was by his. He transformed the cultural perception (at least in movies) of Asians as short, near-sighted, weak individuals suitable for only comedic roles, to people of strength and dignity. His most notable contributions are of course, the popularization of Martial Arts in the West and 5 movies which showcase his stunning talent, natural charisma, and deep intensity. His influence is both multicultural and transgenerational; I still remember that as a kid, the catchphrase my friends and I used when we wanted to incorporate martial arts (or our version of it ☺) in our play time was 'let's fight Bruce Lee'! Not karate. Not Judo. Not kung Fu. Bruce Lee.

Unfortunately, this epitome of physical fitness passed on before he turned 33, leaving shockwaves and a huge gap in the world of movies. But like true legends, his influence and impact continue to live on. His philosophy of 'be water' – being adaptable to any fighting style – continues to inspire many, including a Hong Kong anti-government protest group.

'Who is the next Bruce Lee?' was possibly the most burning question among fans and movie buffs in the years following his untimely demise in 1973. Many candidates, lookalikes and fight-a-likes stepped forward, hoping to accede to the throne vacated by the 'Little Dragon'.

All of them failed.

One of the more well-known action heroes around that period who was touted as the next Bruce Lee, was a young man called Jackie Chan. A former stuntman (who had actually shared screen time with Lee, as a stuntman and extra), he'd had a number of movies under his belt - several of which were fairly popular - but found that, like every other hopeful, he was constantly over-shadowed by a dead man.

But one day, Jackie realized something important: although he started out wanting to be the next Bruce Lee like everyone else, he couldn't be the next Bruce Lee...for the simple reason that there had already **been** a Bruce Lee! You couldn't be more Bruce than Bruce. He decided, instead, to be Jackie Chan.

And that was when everything changed.

He wrote and produced movies which focused on the elaborate fight scenes, daring stunts and slapstick humor which became both his trademark and his winning formula: when you watched a Jackie Chan movie, you more or less knew what to expect. Chan is now a legend in his own right (with over a 100 movies to his credit) as well as a household name...because he decided to stop being a poor version of someone else and the best version of himself.

This is the heart of Innovation.

Too many of us latch on to a successful idea and want to copy it because we think it's sympathetic magic: if we do exactly what they did, we must get the same results! But nothing could be further from the truth. Imitation stifles your personal creativity: when you envy another person's gift due to the success they have had, you copy them so you could have that success for your own...but in doing so you forget a critical thing: you have **your own gift**, by imitating that of another, you are neglecting yours.

The same is true of business as it is of individuals.

This shouldn't be surprising; businesses are run by **people.** It is the quality of their thoughts, mindsets and attitudes that translate into how they run the companies under their control. This boils down to YOU. What is your mindset? Are you driven so badly by the need to beat your competition at their own game that you focus on what they do so you could copy it and do better?

There's actually a place for a form of imitation: when someone is able to complete a process faster and better than you could; the wise thing to do is to learn how they did it which could involve adapting their material, strategy or approach.

But when you constantly and consistently imitate, you are dampening that spark of creativity that you have.

If you want to succeed as an Entrepreneur, you must constantly challenge yourself to be creative. Don't latch on to trends; trailblaze. You must develop the unique vision that caused you to go into business and continue to challenge yourself. Don't be satisfied with a measure of success. You can do more; you can be more. Don't envy the success of others; learn from them, but don't copy them.

Don't Imitate; Emulate.

CHAPTER 5

THE NUMBERS: FINANCE & ACCOUNTING

"The number one problem in today's generation and economy is the lack of financial literacy." - Alan Greenspan

Ah, the numbers.

For some entrepreneurs, Finance & Accounting is the most exciting aspect of business, for others, the most frightening!

Not that I don't understand the anxiety of those of us in the 'frightened' camp. In wrong - rather, ill-equipped – hands, finance can be a nightmare, accounting a jumble of numbers that make no sense whatsoever. This is certainly not helped by the high-flying terms you may have heard from some of your accounting friends, bankers and investing professionals: Equity, Debt, Cost of Capital, Assets, Liabilities, ROA, ROE, ROI, Cash Flow, Working Capital....

What?

What??

What???

But let not your hearts be troubled, you can get through this☺.

Don't get me wrong though; I'm not saying that Finance & Accounting is *that* easy to grasp (not all at once), but it certainly is not the horror movie you may have thought it was. As with any subject, it can be mastered. Here are two key things to keep in mind when dealing with the numbers in business:

- Ease or complexity will depend on your perspective - your approach to the subject and your willingness to learn.
- As a business owner or entrepreneur, a working knowledge of finance and accounting is **critical.**

I'll share a personal story that illustrates the importance of the first point, and then we'll discuss the significance of the second.

The bulk of my working experience as an employee was gained in Finance, particularly in the areas of Performance Management, Financial reporting, and analysis. These areas, like virtually any in Finance, require at least an intermediate knowledge of Excel spreadsheets but more importantly, the ability to understand how numbers work, how to put them together, how to dissect them and how to use them in various ways to achieve a varied set of objectives.

But the thing is…I didn't start as a finance professional, or with a finance degree, not even a business or numerate degree. My first degree happens to be in English Language (a subject I always had a natural bent for) but I found myself working in Banking with the first several years of my career spent in Banking Operations; now up to that point, my experience of Excel spreadsheets was limited to carrying out basic arithmetic computations and learning one or two functions that simplified processes; I remember discovering the auto sum function and thinking I had become an Excel guru.

Smh.

A few months later, I found myself redeployed to the Performance Management Unit, standing before the Department Head, an astute gentleman with a raspy voice (and large tummy☺). He looked me up and down:

Him: So! You've been redeployed to me. How good is your knowledge of Excel?
Me (trying to sound modest): oh, I'm pretty good Sir. Probably around 60% efficacy.
Him: Oh, that's great! We'll be doing a lot of Excel work. I expect you to use VLOOKUP. You know VLOOKUP, right…?
Me (after a confused pause): VLOOKUP? Er…no, not really Sir…
Him: Hmm. Oh. Ok…well…at least you can use MID, right?
Me (starting to break into a slight sweat): um…well…no, not really Sir….
Him (no longer smiling): Surely…surely…you must know CONCATENATE…
Me (thoroughly frightened): No Sir!!!

Him: So, WHAT do you know?

And that was my 'auspicious' entry into Finance! The first week for me was a confused mess of all sorts of numbers, lines, rows, and columns; by the end of that week, I was just about ready to quit! It got so bad I actually developed a fever and was away from work a couple of days (I think I really did have an actual bad dream involving spreadsheets, VLOOKUP, MID, CONCATENATE...and woke up in a cold sweat☺). Oh, it was *bad.*

But then something happened. At some point between my fever, nightmares, and recovery, I had a thought. And it was this: I am going to learn this stuff.

Bam! That was it.

I don't know exactly how or why I suddenly had that thought. Perhaps it's because I hate to fail at anything; perhaps I didn't want to disappoint my astute, raspy-voiced, big tummy-d boss; perhaps I felt challenged by the scope of the work...or perhaps it was all 3. Whatever the underlying motive was, it resulted in that single thought. And when I had that thought, I decided to act on it. I went back to work determined to learn and conquer the job...and about 10 years later I found myself appointed as Chief Finance Officer and Finance Business Partner of the most critical Division in the Bank, advising Team Leads, Group Heads and Divisional Heads on finance and business performance management, using the same Excel I once dreaded.

True story.

Yes, I know that you're an Entrepreneur and not a CFO-wannabe☺ but there are insights from this story that are of benefit to you:

- Do not underestimate the power of a Thought. More than most people I think, Entrepreneurs can appreciate the power of an idea. Your business is the fruit of a thought you once had, after all. When dealing with numbers, all you need do is amplify the thought that you can do it, and you will. Henry Ford said "whether you think you can, or you think you can't – you're right". And he was spot on. But then again, he was only distilling this accuracy; the original truth had been given to us in the Bible millennia ago: "as a man thinketh in his heart, so is he" (Proverbs 23:7). Just saying.
- When you make up your mind and decide to do something, you cannot be stopped.

The importance of the earlier point on the need for business owners to have a working knowledge of Finance is that without this knowledge, without this 'Light', there is no way you will know or understand how well (or not) your business is doing. How do you know if the decisions you're making are the right ones? How do you know when you need to invest? How do you know if you have enough funds to run the business at any given period? How do you know if you are running a profitable concern? How do you plan for future business cycles?

All these questions are answered through the numbers!

You can hire an accountant for this stuff, you say? Sure. I'm not asking you to be a full-time accountant, but YOU are the owner of the business. Even when your accountant reports to you on the financials, you need to be savvy enough to understand what he's saying; not to mention when you must talk to potential investors. I think you'll agree it's best that you don't have a 'what are you going on about' look on your face during those periods☺.

Finance is a vast field with various categories and sub-categories, some of them esoteric. However, for you, the importance of Finance is in how it applies to your business and how you can develop the ability to read and analyze numbers to make decisions.

Let's jump into it, shall we?'

Understanding and Analyzing Financial Statements

There's a wealth of information out there on the components and analysis of Financial Statements, available at a click. But why don't we approach things informally, without getting overly technical? Once you imbibe the basics, the critical building blocks, you can gain further insight through additional research.

Financial Statements provide holistic information on the business - **any** business. Through them you get to have statistics on the liquidity, funding, and revenue of your business, among other valuable data. There are basically 3 of such statements; these financial statements are interrelated and together, provide a composite view of the financial health of the business.

The Statement of Cash Flow
'Cash is King'.

Ever heard that one before? For Business Owners especially, this is an indisputable truth. What runs your business? How do you purchase goods? How do you pay salaries? What do you use to service your loans? Do you realize that on paper, your business could be profitable, but you could **still** end up closing shop 3 months later due to poor cash flow?

Cash. Cash. Cash.

So, who gave Cash his crown and why does he deserve the honor?

Well, without cash actively running through your business, the simple fact is that it's as good as dead. Cash is the lifeblood of the business. Your business needs cash.

It can't survive without cash. We can say this in 100 different ways…but I'm sure you get the drift☺.

Obviously, this means that a key priority is to ensure we have enough cash in the business, efficiently taking care of different activities and that more importantly, we have enough of it left over. We want to ensure that we are a viable (and valuable) going concern.

The financial statement which directly addresses the issues concerning cash is called the **Statement of Cash Flow.** Cash Flow refers to the total amount of cash that is transferred in and out of a business, and how this inward and outward flow affects Liquidity (which is basically the ability of a business to cover obligations with cash, or items that can be quickly converted to cash).

How does this work in real, practical terms?
Say you've started out as an Agripreneur and desire to sell homegrown produce at affordable prices in your local community. At the beginning of the season, you invested some personal savings and took a loan from a friend (to be repaid with interest), bought a small Farmer's Stand, a tractor and tools, seeds, fertilizer, bags, and utilities, set up shop and got right down to work. At the end of the season your land yielded a bountiful harvest and customers, attracted by word of mouth, have flocked in droves to buy your fruits and vegetables.

To effectively compete against local supermarkets, you set your prices at about 50% of theirs, making you even more attractive to customers. The demand is so high you've had to hire several people to help you sell and run your stand/shop. It's exciting to witness the popularity of your business (food after all is a permanently essential commodity), the cash is pouring in and you dream about the fat bank account that's just accumulating.

D-Day arrives and you're up, eager to check your account balance☺. The purpose of the business was to impact lives and not amass profit; but you've worked hard and deserve to see a healthy balance. However, as you check your total balance, your smile of anticipation slowly turns into a frown. Wait a minute...how come the cash is so small? Hundreds of people purchased stuff from you, didn't they? Where's all the cash? Where's all the moolah? Who moved your cheese! ☹

Unfortunately, this is a situation all too familiar to hundreds (if not thousands) of startups. Business seems to be going well and you're making great sales but at the end of the period, you just don't seem to have as much cash as you think you should or worse, no cash at all. You're left puzzled, the issues of life boiled down to a single question: where did all the cash go?

Well, the Statement of Cash Flow provides the answer!

Let's look at how this Statement would work based on the above scenario: the first thing to do (after drying your eyes) is organize all your information based on **inflows** (funds received into the business aka what put cash in your pocket) and **outflows** (expenses you incurred in the course of running the business aka what took cash out of your pocket). It goes without saying that proper records of all inflows and outflows needed to have been maintained (an Excel sheet would do…hey, you could even use VLOOKUP ☺).

Here's how an arrangement of cash inflows and outflows might look using our agripreneur model (we'll stick with dollars for all examples):

Scenario 1.1. Agripreneur Farm Stand, Cash Flows:
First Growing Season

Outflows	$
Seed	1,000
Fertilizer	1,500
Salaries	20,000
Stand	5,000
Tools (including small tractor)	10,000
Supplies (Bags)	1,000
Utilities	2,000
Loan (repaid)	10,000
Others (interest on Loan)	2,000
Total	**52,500**
Inflows	
Personal Savings	5,000
Loan Received	10,000
Sales	40,000
Total	**55,000**
Net Cash Inflow	**2,500**

Voila, a Cash Flow Statement!

This is a simplified and informal representation, but it shows the basic information you require: cash inflows, cash outflows and net cash (the difference between total inflows and outflows).

The final figure in the above example is tagged 'Net Cash Inflow' because it is a **positive** figure, indicating that total inflows were greater than outflows during the period (the reverse would be net cash outflow). We are also able to understand why the available cash at the end of the period was not as much as expected: although sales were pretty decent and resulted in a healthy credit balance, total expense incurred during the period was more than sales and but for the personal savings invested and the loan, we would have ended with a negative figure (net cash outflow).

But before we immediately assume that the business is somehow deficient, and we need to drive sales or cut down expenses let's take this a step further. We can see what the inflows and outflows are, but what would be more insightful would be to understand how these flows relate to the business, based on the various activities which occurred. This way we can appreciate how the cash that flows through the business was used, and which activity caused us to spend more...and why.

Rearranging the cash flow based on the above would then look like this:

Scenario 1.2. Agripreneur Farm Stand, Statement of Cash Flows
by activity: First Growing Season

	$	$
Cash Flow : Operating Activities		
Inflow from Sales		40,000
Outflows		
Seed	1,000	
Fertilizer	1,500	
Salaries	20,000	
Supplies	1,000	
Utilities	2,000	
Others (interest on Loan)	2,000	-27,500
Net Cash from Operations		**12,500**
Cash Flow : Investing Activities		
Outflows		
Farm Stand	5,000	
Tools/Tractor	10,000	
Net Cash from Investments		-15,000
Cash Flow : Financing Activities		
Inflows		
Personal Savings	5,000	
Loan	10,000	
Outflows		
Loan Repayment (principal)	-10,000	
Net Cash from Financing		5,000
Net Cash Inflow		**2,500**

Looks much more professionally organized doesn't it?
This is a proper Statement of Cash Flow. It's not difficult
to prepare; all we did was take the same information in
the earlier version and re-group the items according to
activity.

Cash flow statements are arranged by Operating, Investing and Financing activity; the key to categorizing cash by activity is in understanding the **purpose** of a given cash inflow or outflow.

Let's relate this assertion to our cash flow statement above.

Cash flow from Operating Activities represents all the cash collected or spent which relate to the core operations of the business. The inflow was from sales of fruits and vegetables, which were generated by the operations of the company while the outflows represented by items such as seed, fertilizer etc. were all directly used in running the business (typical daily business expenses). So, in grouping your cash flow by operating activity, identify all cash items in your records which relate with directly running **day-to-day** business operations. The difference between inflows and outflows in this category is the net cash from operations.

Cash under Investment activity relates to items used in **investing** in the business for the benefit of maximizing your assets (we'll talk more about assets in a bit) to increase income. Think of how you invest in the stock market or in financial assets like Treasury Bills/Bonds; the purpose of doing this is basically to increase your net worth right? In the same way, there are investment activities you undertake for the business to generate a future return or income. Cash items under the

Investment Activity category tend to be outflows as we typically must spend cash when investing. The cash spent on the tractor in the above model is an investment activity and not an operating activity; although the tractor is used in operations, the **purpose** of buying it was to benefit many seasons of operations and generate greater produce which eventually translates to more cash. So, whenever you are unsure about an item which could seem classifiable under more than one activity, you can solve the problem by ascertaining **the objective** of the inflow or outflow.

The final category of financing activity refers to cash received or spent to **finance** (fund) the business. The Financing activities in the agripreneur model represent funds generated to set up the business and get it going. So, the personal savings and loan from the friend were financing **inflows** while the repayment of the loan was a **financing outflow.** On the other hand, the **interest** on the loan was repaid from the **operations** of the business which is why it is captured as an operating (rather than a financing) activity.

Putting it all together, our cash flow statement clearly shows us that the reason total net cash at the end of the period was not as much as expected was **not** due to poor cash flow from operations but because of major investments (equipment) which significantly reduced the net cash position.

By using the Statement of Cash Flow, we are able to gauge the sufficiency of the cash position of the business, constantly determine and monitor its liquidity and solvency as well as see the impact of various cash activities in the bank balance.

The Income Statement

Our second financial statement is the Income Statement (also known as the Profit or Loss Statement or P or L). The primary purpose of the Income Statement is to reveal how **profitable** the business is. Naturally, this is important for you to know because you want to gauge how well your business is doing. In understanding the Income Statement, the basic rule to bear in mind is that for your business to show a positive net income (i.e. profitability), the total revenue or earnings generated by the business must exceed total expense.

If that sounds similar to how the Statement of Cash Flow works, here's the difference between the two: the cash flow statement **matches cash inflows and outflows**; the Income Statement **matches effort and accomplishment**.

Let's break that down further: earlier I mentioned that a business could be profitable but still wind up shutting down due to poor cash flow. How's that possible? This phenomenon stems from what is called the **basis of accounting**, which is simply the method (basis) selected to record revenues and expenses in the Income Statement.

There are 2 methods or bases of accounting: cash and accrual; the difference between the two is the **timing** of when sales (revenue) and costs/purchases (expenses) are recorded. When money changes hands instantly (i.e. via immediate cash payments) and you record them as soon as they occur, this method of recognizing them is **Cash Accounting**. In other words, cash accounting recognizes income and expense only when cash payments are made.

On the other hand, **Accrual Accounting** is based on accretion; this means that revenue and expenses are recorded when they are earned and billed - not when they are paid. Here's an example of how this works:

Let's take revenue as a result of sales in our agripreneur model: your customer came to buy some fruits and vegetables from your stand worth $500 and paid you immediately in **cash**. In recording this sale in your books, you would use the cash accounting method. However, if the customer bought the produce but promised to pay in a fortnight or the following month, you could only record this sale under the **accrual** basis because the sale was not done via cash. Your account is not credited with the $500 until the customer actually pays; however, on **the books** you have made a sale and earned revenue!

Now, if the entire $40,000 earned in our agripreneur business came from deferred (accrued) payments from customers who for some reason or other did not meet up with their promises to pay cash as at when due, we would obviously be in a whole lot of trouble!

Accrual accounting provides a better picture or view of the financial state of the business; cash accounting gives a better picture of the actual funds in your account. Because the accrual concept is the more preferred accounting basis, the income statement could show a business that is profitable but low on cash. **This** is why businesses can be profitable but still close down: on the books they record healthy revenues but the actual cash in their possession does not match up to paper earnings; consequently cash flow is insufficient and they are eventually unable to continue operations.

Sad, isn't it? ☹

The above underscores why the individual components of financial statements should not be reviewed or analyzed in isolation: the statement of cash flow provides pertinent information the income statement does not (and vice versa).

Another integral difference which distinguishes the Income Statement from the Cash Flow statement is that it is able to record items which did not translate into actual cash flows but which need to be recognized to provide a near as accurate view of the business as possible.

For instance, in our agripreneur cash flow statement we had captured the actual cash outflow for the equipment (tools and tractor) purchased as investment activities. What the cash flow statement did **not** show was the expense related to the equipment. It also did not capture the additional sum of $2,500 owed the fertilizer shop (we had actually purchased $4,000 worth of fertilizer but paid $1,500 at the start of the business, so the cash flow only captured what was actually paid) as well as a further $1,000 owed a more experienced colleague in the same business in another part of the country who had flown over to render some much needed consultation advice on organic farming and business operations.

These expenses are legitimate and need to be accounted for to give a proper view of the profitability of business operations; but the cash flow statement was unable to factor in these items as they were not outright cash payments.

Enter the Income Statement.
Let's start with accounting for the stand and equipment: before purchasing these items we had ascertained how many years these investments would benefit business operations (this is known as the useful life of the asset); our findings revealed that we could

expect to use the stand for 4 years, while the tractor and tools would yield 10 years of benefits.

Great; but how do we capture this information and show its impact on the bottom line of the business?

We do this based on the concept of **Depreciation.** Depreciation enables us account for the costs associated with such assets (again, more on assets shortly) on the Income Statement during a specific period (the period we are examining). The concept of depreciation is based on the fact that as assets are used up, their value goes down (think about how a car you bought worth $100,000 is only worth 50% of that amount a year or two later). In accounting, the original investments in such assets need to be allocated to the periods they were used (aka 'wear and tear').

Let's demonstrate that: the total original investment in the equipment was $10,000 and we have determined that they have a useful asset life of 10 years. So, what is the cost of depreciation for the period we are reviewing? It is the cost of the investment **for that period**. In other words, if we were looking at our Income Statement for the year, the depreciation cost of the equipment would be $1,000 (one tenth of original cost); if for a month then it would be the annual depreciation cost divided by 12 ($83.33).

In this scenario the growing season covers a period of one year so our Income Statement would show $1,000 as the depreciation cost of the equipment while the depreciation cost of the stand would be $1,250 (i.e. original investment cost of $5,000/useful asset life of 4 years).

The $1,000 fee to the Consultant should be recorded as a separate expense line (or tagged as Other/Miscellaneous Expense with a note to specify it relates to the Consultant). Since all other expenses have already been paid via cash, we now have a complete picture of our expenses (efforts) which we can match to the revenue (accomplishments) and arrive at the net income (net income = revenue – expenses).

Do you get it? You do? Wonderful. See? I told you this stuff isn't that hard☺. So, let's have a look at our Income Statement:

Scenario 1.3. Agripreneur Farm Stand, Income Statement: First Growing Season

	$	$
Sales (Revenue)		40,000
Expenses		
Seed	-1,000	
Fertilizer	-4,000	
Salaries	-20,000	
Supplies (Bags)	-1,000	
Utilities	-2,000	
Others (interest on Loan)	-2,000	
Consultant	-1,000	
Depreciation		
Equipment	-1,000	
Farmer's Stand	-1,250	
Total	**-33,250**	**40,000**
Net Income		**6,750**

So we have total revenue, represented by sales and total expense including cash payments and depreciation. The difference between the two is the Net Income.

Essentially the Income Statement shows the revenue earned from sales, and the costs which produced those sales. You can see from the above that the Net Income figure is quite different from the Net Cash Inflow in the Statement of Cash Flow position. While the cash flow shows us the cash received or spent, the Income Statement considers the cost of the major items invested in for the period we are looking at. So, for the first year in the life of our agripreneur business we have a net cash inflow of $2,500 while we recorded a profit of $6,750.

Bravo☺.

The Balance Sheet

And now for the third member of the Financial Statement trinity☺.

To complete our 360 degree view of the financial state of the business, we need to have a picture of what the business owns and what it owes, as well as the status of the investments that you as the business owner, made into the business.

Why is this critical?

The Cash Flow Statement will give you a picture of your cash balances and liquidity but will not show you how profitable your business is. The Income Statement will show you how profitable you are but usually only at the end of the operating period. At different occasions you will need to have a snapshot of the business **as it is** at that specific point in time, which you can quickly assess and from which you can derive the above information – what you own, what you owe and your investment as the business owner.

The Financial Statement that provides this information is the Balance Sheet, and it contains 3 basic (but vital) components:

Assets

Assets are the resources owned or controlled by the business, which are used to generate a future profit (either in the short or long term) and attend to obligations. Simply stated, any item your business owns which puts money in your pocket either through its sale or use is an **Asset.** Assets provide the answer to the question: "how much do I have?"

Let's refer to the items listed in the cash flow statement for our agripreneur business: what are the items that, based on the above definition, can be classified as Assets? The first is Cash. We own or control a net cash balance of $2,500 which we can use to generate income, through investments; we can also use this cash to attend to some of the obligations of the business as they arise. The Farmer's Stand and Equipment are also assets as we use them in the operations of the business to generate more produce (which when sold, generates income for the business); if push came to shove we could also sell these items for cash.

In recording Assets in the financial statement, we list them in order of **liquidity** i.e. how quickly they can be converted to cash. Liquidity then forms the basis of differentiating between **Current** and **Long-Term (or Fixed) Assets.** A Current Asset is any asset that can be sold or used within a period of one year and which enables day-to-day operations (expenses or investments of the business, to keep it up and running), while a Long Term/Fixed Asset can only be sold or used after a period of one year. Fixed Assets are also called PPE (Property, Plant and Equipment) and are used in the manufacture of the product or service a business is involved in. The Depreciation concept plays out on Fixed Assets rather than Current Assets as the latter cannot be depreciated due to their short-term nature.

So again, looking at the assets in the agripreneur model, Cash would be a Current Asset (because you can use it immediately, and definitely under one year) while the Farmer's Stand and Equipment are Long-Term/Fixed Assets because they can be used by the business for several years and are unlikely to be sold under a year.

On the Balance Sheet, Current Assets are recorded at their face value while Fixed Assets are listed at their Purchase Cost, minus depreciation. In other words, Fixed Assets are not shown at their current estimated value but at the price originally paid for them **minus** depreciation cost (which accounts for the decline in the value of the asset during the period). For example, in recording the Farmer's Stand on the Balance Sheet we would list it at its original cost ($5,000) less its depreciation cost for that period ($1,000); as Fixed Items continue to depreciate, their listing on the Balance Sheet changes to accommodate the increase in Depreciation Cost.

Current and Fixed Assets together give you a complete picture of all resources (Total Assets) owned by your business and what they represent in terms of value.

While this is great to know, something is missing: perhaps you're asking exactly how these assets are financed or funded by the business.

Liabilities

We briefly touched on Liabilities in our earlier conversation on Structuring the Business and generally defined a liability as an obligation to pay, which is correct. In the more specific business finance sense, a liability is a commitment to pay out an asset (usually cash) to your creditor (basically anyone you owe money). Liabilities answer the question "how much do I owe?"

Looking at the agripreneur model once again, it should be pretty easy to pick out our liabilities. Ask yourself what items represent what is owed. You got it? The Fertilizer Store and the Consultant! All other expenses had already been settled by cash, so you don't owe anything else asides these two. They are there, waiting to be sorted; they are the obligations you will have to pay at some point. They are Liabilities.

As with Assets, Liabilities are also divided into Current and Long Term, based on how soon they are due. Any liability due to be paid in one year or less is a current liability and liabilities that are due to be paid over one year are Long Term Liabilities.

For our current example, both liabilities are due within the next growing season (1 year) and so are both Current Liabilities. If on the other hand, the $10,000 loan that was taken out to boost the startup capital of the business was due to be repaid over 2 or 3 years, the unpaid balance would be listed as a Long Term Liability (debt).

You know your business is healthy when your total assets exceed your total liabilities, because it means that you 'own' more than you 'owe'; if push came to shove and you had to settle all your obligations at that moment, you would **still** have resources left over.

Before we leave Liabilities though, let's go over an important concept. Net total Assets (i.e. where Total Assets exceed Total Liabilities) is an indication of financial health, as I just explained. But note that this includes Fixed Assets which we now know are assets which cannot be realized within a year.

So, let's pose another question: how do you ascertain if your business is healthy in the **short term**? What tells you if your operational efficiency, liquidity, and ability to meet your liability obligations are on point?

Answer: Working Capital!

Working Capital is basically what you get when you net off your Current Assets and your Current Liabilities. Remember that these two refer to assets/liabilities that can be realized/must be paid within a year; so this gives you a clear idea of what your short-term financial health is.

A negative working capital (Current Liabilities more than Current Assets) shows you at once that you're headed for trouble, as you are not able to meet your obligations should they all crystallize within the year. This is a key metric that lenders and investors look for when reviewing your financials so you must ensure that your Working Capital is positive per time.

Moving on, let's look at the last link in the Balance Sheet. There is a reason why the Balance Sheet was given that name…after all, something called a balance sheet should balance☺.

Owners' Equity

I just explained that your business can be said to be healthy when your Total Assets exceed your Total Liabilities. The figure you get when you deduct all you owe from all you own is called the **Net Worth** i.e. what the business is worth after all liabilities have been paid off. But, what does this have to do with the Balance Sheet concept?

Because it is the Net Worth that balances the equation!

The net worth of the business is also called **Owner's Equity**. Sound confusing? Ok, let's look back at the Statement of Cash Flow: remember personal savings of $5,000 was invested as start-up capital? That's what is called a **Direct Investment** by the owner into the business and represents the equity held by the owner. That's not all though: take a look at the Income Statement again. We see that the business generated a positive net income of $6,750 at the end of the period. Great. But that's still not the end of that story - the net income is a positive income flow to the business, because the business was operated profitably.

As we have learned, Revenues bring assets into the business while Expenses flow assets out of the business; so if revenues are greater than expenses, you get income which increases assets (this is beneficial to the business owner who **owns** the assets). An increase in the owner's assets then means that the owner's **equity** has grown (decrease means the owner's equity decreased); an increase in owner's equity resulting from profitable operations (when revenues exceed expenses) is called **Retained Earnings** (because it represents the income that is left at the close of a period of business operations, which can then be reinvested to fund business growth). Direct Investment and Retained Earnings = total Owner's Equity. The key difference is that direct investment occurs at the beginning of the business while retained earnings come at the end of a period.

How does Owner's Equity balance the Balance Sheet then?

The formula for the Balance Sheet is Total Assets = Total Liabilities + Owner's Equity. This means that for your Balance Sheet to Balance, your total assets must equal your total liabilities and owner's equity. Put another way, whatever the Owner's Equity is (negative or positive) when added to Total Liabilities, will equal Total Assets, or when you subtract your Total Liabilities from Total Assets what you have left is your Net Worth.

Putting all of this together, here's what the Balance Sheet for the agripreneur model would look like:

**Example 1.4. Agripreneur Farm Stand, Balance Sheet:
End of the First Growing Season**

Assets ($)			
Current Assets			
Cash			2,500
Long-term Assets			
Farm Stand at cost	5,000		
Less: Accumulated Depreciation	-1,250	3,750	
Tractor/Tools at cost	10,000		
Less: Accumulated Depreciation	-1,000	9,000	12,750
Total Assets			**15,250**

Liabilities ($)		
Current Liabilities		
Payable to Fertilizer Store	2,500	
Payable to Consultant	1,000	
Total Liabilities		3,500

Owner's Equity ($)		
Original Investment	5,000	
Retained Earnings	6,750	
Total owner's equity		11,750
Total liabilities and owner's equity		**15,250**

This shows the Total Assets of the business classified into Current and Fixed Assets, the Total Liabilities (which are both current) and the Owner's Equity of $11,750, comprising the original investment (personal savings) of $5,000 and Retained Earnings (net income) of $6,750 from the first year of the business. When you add the Owner's Equity of $11,750 to the Total Liabilities of

$3,500, you get $15,250: the same figure as your Total Assets.

Your Balance Sheet is Balanced!

The Balance Sheet is obviously a very important financial statement and needs to be properly understood. Once you do, you can easily review it and derive all the necessary information on what your business owns and owes, and what your equity as the business owner is.

But without understanding the components of the Balance Sheet, you will not be able to master the finances of your business.

Worse, even while you are making sales and cash is flowing in, on the other hand you could have debt which could pile up and eventually overtake your assets if you are not careful. When you have and understand this essential information however, you will be able to transact business confidently and know exactly where your business stands.

There you have it.

I hope it's sufficiently clear that as an Entrepreneur, you need to understand Financial Statements and how they work. If you apply for a loan for your business (Debt financing), the lender will naturally ask to see your Financial Statements (typically the Income Statement and Balance Sheet); in Equity Financing, Investors are more likely to ask for a Statement of Cash Flow. When questions arise from either of these scenarios, they will be directed at you (not your accountant☺).

You need to understand all three financial statements to make informed decisions for the short- and long-term survival of your company.

Forecasting

As a new business, you will at some point require additional funding. But unless you can guarantee that significant sums of funds will miraculously drop into your business from above☺, this additional funding is going to come from one of two external sources (or maybe both): Debt or Equity.

Debt financing is when you **borrow** the money that you need; the most familiar example of this is a loan from a bank or financing outfit. This loan (if granted) would then be used by your business for whatever purpose you required it for. On your Balance Sheet, it would be represented as a Debt liability which would either be current or long term depending on the tenor (the length/period) of the loan – if within a year it is a current liability, if more than a year it is long term. On the Income Statement, the interest on the loan would form part of your expenses while on your Cash Flow Statement the principal inflow would be a Finance Activity. As you pay down on the loan, the repayment of the principal would be Finance Activity outflow while the **interest** repayment would be an Operational Activity outflow. So Debt financing obviously impacts all 3 of your financial statements.

Equity financing on the other hand is when an external party **invests** in the business by exchanging funds for part ownership of the business. Unlike debt where you have to repay a loan, what the investor gets in return is a share of the business (meaning that his investment will be captured under Owner's Equity as he is also an owner in the business).

While this is nice information to have, where am I going with this you're probably asking?

The point is this: irrespective of which financing option you choose, any lender or investor is going to ask for your financial statements. If you were an already established business, you would start by producing the financials of the last 3-5 years so they can see how you have been operating. But you are a new business and so won't have historical financials. What will they ask for then?

Your **forecast** financial statements.

With a good working knowledge of financial statements, you can forecast and translate future predictions of your business into **pro forma statements,** which are basically the financial representation of management predictions; in other words, the expected financial state of the business after the forecast period.

Forecast financial statements are an essential part of your Business Plan, which is your pitch to potential lenders and/or investors. Before they part with their money, either of these parties will definitely ask to see your financials for the future. If you are unable to prepare (or understand) the information, there is a strong probability that you will not get the additional funding you require.

How do you prepare a forecast of your financial statements?

First, you must have an idea of where you are currently. Our conversation on financial statements was geared to have you develop yours, so before you start forecasting you should have your current statements handy.

Next, you develop what we call **assumptions.** These refer to the expectations you have of the future trend for the business; naturally, they must be as realistic and as grounded as possible, backed up by hard facts or intelligent research. For instance, you can't assume that in the following year your revenue will grow from $40,000 to $40,000,000 without showing how or why this could be possible!

Assumptions or 'drivers' can be plugged into different scenarios that you can develop based on facts or research analysis you would have done, as well as decisions that are based on your projections for business growth.

In planning for future financial periods using pro forma financial statements, you are estimating what the financial position of the business is likely to be when you implement your expansion plan; this helps you organize your plan and present the expected results in a clear and logical manner that potential lenders/investors can relate to.

Let's use our agripreneur model to develop assumptions for projected changes in business operations and then review the impact of these assumptions on our financials.

Assumptions

- We will generate a higher yield of produce and increase our prices to 90% of local supermarket prices (from 50%), based on continued patronage since prices are still favorably competitive.
- To widen customer base, we plan to purchase a truck to transport the produce to farmer's markets within our vicinity.

Business Impact

- Sales will grow to $130,000: to achieve this projected income, we intend to plant more to generate more produce (in addition to the planned 40% hike in prices).

- Seed expense will grow to $3,000: due to the planned expansion; we will purchase 3x more seed than the last growing season.
- Fertilizer expense will grow to $8,000: we are switching to having fertilizer delivered from the stores.
- Salaries will grow to $30,000: we will employ additional staff as well as a driver for the truck.
- Utilities will grow to $2,200: only marginal growth anticipated as the Farmer's Stand is large enough to support the projected increase in sales.
- Fuel/Insurance Expense of $4,000: fuel and insurance for the truck.
- Depreciation will grow by $6,000: the truck will cost $40,000 and has been determined to have a useful asset life of 6.7 years.

Based on the above assumptions, we can forecast Cash flow, Income Statement and Balance Sheet for the second growing season:

Scenario 1.5. Agripreneur Farm Stand, Projected Statement of Cash Flows: Second Growing Season

	$	$
Cash Flow : Operating Activities		
Inflow from Sales		130,000
Outflows		
Seed	3,000	
Fertilizer	10,500	
Salaries	30,000	
Supplies	1,500	
Utilities	2,200	
Fuel/Insurance - Truck	4,000	
Consultant	1,000	
		-52,200
Net Cash from Operations		**77,800**
Cash Flow : Investing Activities		
Outflows		
Truck	40,000	
Net Cash from Investments		-40,000
Net Cash Inflow		**37,800**
Beginning Cash Balance		2,500
Net Cash Inflow		**40,300**

Scenario 1.6. Agripreneur Farm Stand, Projected Income Statement: Second Growing Season

	$	$
Sales (Revenue)		130,000
Expenses		
Seed	-3,000	
Fertilizer	-8,000	
Salaries	-30,000	
Supplies (Bags)	-1,500	
Fuel/Insurance - Truck	-4,000	
Utilities	-2,200	
Depreciation		
Truck	-6,000	
Equipment	-1,000	
Farmer's Stand	-1,250	
Total	-56,950	130,000
Net Income		**73,050**

Scenario 1.7. Agripreneur Farm Stand, Projected Balance Sheet: Second Growing Season

Assets ($)			
Current Assets			
Cash			40,300
Long-term Assets			
Truck	40,000		
Less: Accumulated Depreciation	-6,000	34,000	
Farm Stand at cost	5,000		
Less: Accumulated Depreciation	-2,500	2,500	
Tractor/Tools at cost	10,000		
Less: Accumulated Depreciation	-2,000	8,000	44,500
Total Assets			**84,800**

Liabilities ($)	
Total Liabilities	0

Owner's Equity ($)		
Beginning Owner's Equity	11,750	
Retained Earnings	73,050	
Total owner's equity		84,800
Total liabilities and owner's equity		**84,800**

We have successfully forecast our prediction for the second growing season!

Let's look at how the assumptions and impact translated into the actual numbers.

- Sales forecast of $130,000 was represented on the Cash Flow Statement as cash inflow from Operating Activities, as well as on the Income Statement as Revenue (this means that we expect projected sales will be cash payments and not accrual).

- Projected increase in costs - Salaries, Fuel/Insurance, Fertilizer, Seed, Supplies and Utilities are all accounted for in cash outflows (Statement of Cash Flow) and Expenses (Income Statement).
- The additional investment of $40,000 for the truck was represented in the Cash Flow as an investment activity, on the Income Statement via increase in Depreciation, and on the Balance Sheet as an additional Fixed Asset.

We can further see how the forecast linked all 3 statements to give us an interrelated report. The significant increase in sales catered for the projected growth in cash flows on both operations and investment activities; no additional financing is expected so there was no inflow or outflow for financing activities (note that our net cash inflow from the initial growing season was represented as the beginning cash balance of the second season).

We forecast that business operations would show an enhanced profitability in the second growing season; majorly due to increased revenues which are expected to sufficiently cover expenses and result in a much higher net income.

The Balance Sheet projections show an expected growth in Asset base, which we expect will be financed solely from Equity as there are no outstanding liabilities (note that Owner's Equity shows a projected improvement due to increased Retained Earnings).

When you can properly forecast your numbers based on sound business assumptions and analysis, you can submit a good financial plan to your potential lender/investor and stand a chance of getting that additional funding!

Cost, Volume and Profit Analysis

Now it's time to understand another essential concept; this concerns the relationship of costs and profits to changes in unit volume.

Perhaps you are introducing a new product and want to know how long it will take the product to break-even. Or perhaps you are worried about the effect fierce competition could have on your bottom line. In either case you need to know how changes in the unit volumes will impact the performance of the product or the profitability of the business.

Say you have been running a fast-food business for a year. Your most profitable product is a special beef burger which is really popular (particularly with the younger generation); as such, you're experiencing satisfactory turnover in sales.

The beef burger is sold at $1.95 and the cost of the ingredients (including packaging) is $0.75. The difference between the price you sell the burger and the cost of its ingredients is $1.20. This figure is called the **contribution.** Why? Because it is the amount from the sale of each burger that contributes toward paying the monthly operating costs of the business.

Remember that you are not just producing and selling the burgers in a vacuum. You employ staff, you pay rent, you have equipment that are steadily depreciating, there are repairs and maintenance of the building and equipment that are done as well as other expenses incurred in the course of running the business on a monthly basis. Although you have positive contribution on each burger, you will need to sell a whole lot of burgers to be a profitable business!

Let's consider monthly costs of the business to be as follows:

Cost Head	$
Salaries	12,000
Rent	3,600
Utilities	2,400
Depreciation - Equipment	1,200
Advertising	2,000
Repairs & Maintenance	1,300
Insurance	700
Miscellaneous	800
Total	**24,000**

If sales of the special beef burger average 1,000 daily (i.e. 30,000 burgers a month), we can then compute the monthly profit as follows:

	$
Sales: 30,000 beef burgers @ $1.95 each	58,500
Cost of Ingredients @ $0.75 each	-22,500
Contribution: 30,000 @ $1.20	**36,000**
Monthly Operating Costs	-24,000
Monthly Profit	**12,000**

But we could also arrive at the same result by just using the contribution approach:

	$
Contribution: 30,000 @ $1.20	**36,000**
Monthly Operating Costs	-24,000
Monthly Profit	**12,000**

Easy Peasy☺

Now let's assume that based on the success of the business, 2 new fast food restaurants have decided to set up shop in your vicinity (as is bound to occur). They have studied your business model and want a piece of the pie, so they develop attractive menus and low prices. What happens under such circumstances? Naturally, your sales will decline as customers will also try out these places.

In this scenario, the effect of competition has reduced average sales of your special beef burger to 800 per day (from 1,000). What happens to your monthly profit?

Using the contribution approach, we can quickly compute that:

	$
Contribution: 24,000 @ $1.20	28,800
Monthly Operating Costs	-24,000
Monthly Profit	**4,800**

A 200-unit reduction in **daily** volume has resulted in a 60% reduction in **monthly** profit!

How did this happen?

Let's work back from the result: Profit dropped by $7,200 (60%). The $7,200 is a result of the drop of 6,000 in monthly sales: from 30,000 units (1,000 per day) to 24,000 units (800 per day) because of competition. Multiply the 6,000 by the contribution per unit of $1.20 and you get $7,200 (the drop in profit).

Using this method, we can go ahead to compute what effect an additional 1,000 drop in sales would have: 1,000 * $1.20 = $1,200. Take it even further: how about if sales dropped by a further 4,000 units. This would be 4,000 * $1.20 = $4,800. In other words, if sales declined by 4,000...bye- bye to your profit!

Put another way, if you only achieved monthly sales of 20,000 your contribution of $24,000 (20,000 * $1.20) would be the same as your operating costs of $24,000. This situation is called the **break-even** point (more on this shortly).

It is therefore critical that if you run a business which is competitive, you **must** understand the relationship between costs and profits to changes in unit volume. It is possible to determine from the start when your product or business will break even once you have correct data on contribution and operating costs.

Here's an example of a spreadsheet you could develop:

Units Sold	Sales @ $1.95	Cost of ing @ $0.75	Contribution	Monthly Opex	Profit (PBT)	Total Cost/Unit	PBT/Unit
1,000	1,950	-750	1,200	-24,000	-22,800	-24.75	-22.80
2,000	3,900	-1,500	2,400	-24,000	-21,600	-12.75	-10.80
3,000	5,850	-2,250	3,600	-24,000	-20,400	-8.75	-6.80
4,000	7,800	-3,000	4,800	-24,000	-19,200	-6.75	-4.80
5,000	9,750	-3,750	6,000	-24,000	-18,000	-5.55	-3.60
6,000	11,700	-4,500	7,200	-24,000	-16,800	-4.75	-2.80
7,000	13,650	-5,250	8,400	-24,000	-15,600	-4.18	-2.23
8,000	15,600	-6,000	9,600	-24,000	-14,400	-3.75	-1.80
9,000	17,550	-6,750	10,800	-24,000	-13,200	-3.42	-1.47
10,000	19,500	-7,500	12,000	-24,000	-12,000	-3.15	-1.20
11,000	21,450	-8,250	13,200	-24,000	-10,800	-2.93	-0.98
12,000	23,400	-9,000	14,400	-24,000	-9,600	-2.75	-0.80
13,000	25,350	-9,750	15,600	-24,000	-8,400	-2.60	-0.65
14,000	27,300	-10,500	16,800	-24,000	-7,200	-2.46	-0.51
15,000	29,250	-11,250	18,000	-24,000	-6,000	-2.35	-0.40
16,000	31,200	-12,000	19,200	-24,000	-4,800	-2.25	-0.30
17,000	33,150	-12,750	20,400	-24,000	-3,600	-2.16	-0.21
18,000	35,100	-13,500	21,600	-24,000	-2,400	-2.08	-0.13
19,000	37,050	-14,250	22,800	-24,000	-1,200	-2.01	-0.06
20,000	**39,000**	**-15,000**	**24,000**	**-24,000**	**0**	**-1.95**	**0.00**
21,000	40,950	-15,750	25,200	-24,000	1,200	-1.89	0.06
22,000	42,900	-16,500	26,400	-24,000	2,400	-1.84	0.11
23,000	44,850	-17,250	27,600	-24,000	3,600	-1.79	0.16
24,000	46,800	-18,000	28,800	-24,000	4,800	-1.75	0.20
25,000	48,750	-18,750	30,000	-24,000	6,000	-1.71	0.24
26,000	50,700	-19,500	31,200	-24,000	7,200	-1.67	0.28
27,000	52,650	-20,250	32,400	-24,000	8,400	-1.64	0.31
28,000	54,600	-21,000	33,600	-24,000	9,600	-1.61	0.34
29,000	56,550	-21,750	34,800	-24,000	10,800	-1.58	0.37
30,000	58,500	-22,500	36,000	-24,000	12,000	-1.55	0.40
31,000	60,450	-23,250	37,200	-24,000	13,200	-1.52	0.43
32,000	62,400	-24,000	38,400	-24,000	14,400	-1.50	0.45
33,000	64,350	-24,750	39,600	-24,000	15,600	-1.48	0.47
34,000	66,300	-25,500	40,800	-24,000	16,800	-1.46	0.49
35,000	68,250	-26,250	42,000	-24,000	18,000	-1.44	0.51
36,000	70,200	-27,000	43,200	-24,000	19,200	-1.42	0.53
37,000	72,150	-27,750	44,400	-24,000	20,400	-1.40	0.55
38,000	74,100	-28,500	45,600	-24,000	21,600	-1.38	0.57
39,000	76,050	-29,250	46,800	-24,000	22,800	-1.37	0.58
40,000	78,000	-30,000	48,000	-24,000	24,000	-1.35	0.60

How Do Costs Work?

Let's start by analyzing the behavior of costs and their relationship to unit volumes. Looking at the above you'll notice that monthly opex (operating expense) stayed at the same level irrespective of unit volume. In other words, OPEX remained **fixed**.

Fixed Costs are costs that remain unchanged with respect to **volume**. It's important to note this distinction but bear in mind that Fixed costs may change for other reasons asides volume. For example, rent or salaries could change due to economic factors that are not controlled by the business. When we describe costs as fixed, we therefore mean that they are only fixed with respect to unit volume.

While they do not respond to volume, Fixed Costs however usually relate to **time** and for this reason are also known as period costs (because they change with the passage of time). For instance, rent and insurance costs are based on fixed amounts incurred annually, so irrespective of if you have zero unit volume you will **still** incur fixed costs (note that some fixed costs like Advertising may not relate to time and are discretionary – at the instance of Management).

On the other hand, we can see that the cost of ingredients is not static but changes in direct proportion to unit volume: while the cost of a single burger is $0.75, the more units are produced and sold, the more the cost. So, cost of ingredients rises (or drops) based on unit volume. Such costs are known as **variable** costs because they vary in relation to volume.

But just like Fixed Costs, Variable Costs are based on a general concept, and there are other reasons that could cause a variation. For example, if the cost of tomatoes rises in the market, this will impact the cost of ingredients and push it up. In this case there is a change in cost because of external reasons, which are not related to unit volumes.

The Total Cost of the product or business is therefore is the addition of Fixed and Variable Costs.

Break-Even Analysis

So how can you predict when your product is likely to break-even? Looking at the above table, we started with 1,000 units which resulted in a loss of $22,800 in the first month. But because Total Costs grew more slowly than sales and sales increased by 1,000 units each month, revenue eventually caught up with and overtook total costs.

As long as total costs exceed revenue the product or business will be in a loss; when the reverse is the case, you earn a profit!

Now, the point where sales revenue met up with total costs (@ 20,000 units) is called the **Break-even** point. At the 20,000-unit volume mark, the revenue is $39,000 and total costs are also $39,000 (variable costs of $15,000 + fixed costs of $24,000). Clearly, unit volumes **less** than

20,000 will result in a loss and unit volumes **more** than 20,000 will give you a profit.

Putting it in formula terms:

Profit = Revenues − Variable Costs − Fixed Costs (or Contribution − Fixed Costs).

We can also compute the breakeven analysis using the data above:

Zero	=	Contribution − Fixed Costs
Contribution	=	Fixed Costs
Contribution per unit	=	Fixed costs/no of units to
break even		
No of units to break even	=	Fixed Costs/contribution per
unit		
	=	$24,000/$1.20
	=	20,000 units

Voila!

From the outset, with information on fixed and variable costs and your unit volumes, you can readily arrive at your break-even point! You can also use this approach in forecasting and answering relevant questions. For example, what would be your break-even point if fixed costs increase to $27,000 a month? Simple: $27,000/$1.20 = **22,500**. How about if you want to know how many units to sell to earn a profit of $6,000 a month (based on current fixed costs)? Piece of cake: $24,000 (fixed costs) + $6,000 (target profit) = $30,000 (new contribution required). Then $30,000 (required contribution)/$1.20 = 25,000 units!

The Cost-Profit-Volume and Break-even analyses are really useful and practical techniques that will help you as a business owner to achieve various goals: whether you are opening a new business and want to ascertain break-even point, achieve a target projection or gauge impact of competition or changes in the economy on the business.

Whew! Finance is pretty vast, isn't it?

Once you familiarize yourself with the concepts and continue practicing on developing your financial statements, forecasting and break-even you'll find that it gets easier...and very possibly, more interesting.

Even exciting☺

CHAPTER 6

FINANCING OPTIONS: CONSIDER ME, A GOOD INVESTMENT

"If you make meaning, you'll make money." – Guy Kawasaki

It takes courage to become an Entrepreneur.

This is one of my principal reasons for writing this book, because there aren't so many people who have the guts to do what you do; you have my admiration and commitment to help you succeed.

But let's face it though: fear is a highly limiting factor. What is the first law of nature? Self-preservation. It takes a certain mindset to quit the stability of a 9 – 5 and go out on your own, especially when the odds are not particularly stacked in your favour. A good deal of the fear surrounding starting a new business boils down to statistics: over **90%** of new businesses fail in the first year of operations, current studies have discovered (although in truth the high mortality rate of startups is hardly a recent phenomenon).

But why do new businesses crash so often...and so early?

Remember that quote about our friend, King Cash? Whatever else you may forget, please don't forget it. Cash IS king...especially for a startup. Inadequate funding and liquidity are two of the major issues which affect businesses early on; when you consider that the path from when you first envision your idea to the point of actually generating revenue is not exactly a short or narrow one, you may appreciate this fact a bit more. Consequently, at virtually every phase of your new business journey, the need for adequate financing will be a recurring decimal.

Since funding is a major requirement and a chief reason new business (any business really) could fail, it's wise to examine the various financing options which you could leverage on to raise that much needed capital.

Self-funding is of course your first option. This is putting your money where your mouth is and essentially placing a bet on yourself. If you aren't willing to invest your own money into starting your business, you really shouldn't be starting one. Bootstrapping, as it's also called, is your equity investment into the business as its owner, and by sowing it you are ensuring that you are tied to the business and committed to its success. Your treasure is where your heart is, as the Good Book says. Note that Self-funding is an indicator of the extent of your dedication to potential investors (and yes, that's a plus ☺).

For external fundraising, there are traditional routes such as debt financing from your nearby bank or microfinance institution or perhaps getting a form of government grant.

But there's more than one way to skin a cat ☺...here are 5 additional ways you can get financing:

- **Crowdfunding**: How cool would it be if a 100 people gave you $100 each, just so you could grow your business? Nice idea right? This is the ethos behind crowdfunding, one of the more recent (and popular) methods of funding a startup. How does it work? Basically, an entrepreneur provides a detailed description of his business on a crowdfunding platform, including essential information such as the goals of the business and how profit would be generated, as well as funding needs and objectives. Investors on the platform review this information and, if they like the business idea, 'invest' in it by pledging to pre-order the product or making or donation. Virtually anyone can contribute money toward helping a business that they really believe in.

    The great thing about Crowdfunding as a funding option is that, asides finance, you can leverage on it to generate attention in your business which essentially helps you market your product. This helps you gauge the sort of demand your product/service could generate in the wider market; no professional investors needed here, just the attention of the average (and not so common) man ☺. However, you ought to bear in mind that regardless of anything else, crowdfunding is still an **investment** option and you will be competing with others to generate funding; clearly, your idea needs to stand out.

- **Angel Investors**: Do you believe in Angels; those invisible and powerful spirit beings who can come to your aid in times of need? No? Ok, how about if someone you didn't know decided to invest that $10,000 you need so badly to get your feet off the ground, even though your business idea is on the far side of risky...would you believe *then?* ☺.

   Angel investors are individuals with surplus cash (usually High Net worth Individuals), interested in investing in newbie businesses. They earned their benevolent prefix through a preparedness to invest in businesses (including those that appear more than a little risky), and a willingness to contribute their skills, expertise, knowledge, and contacts (in addition to capital) in assisting the business scale. These are hands-on investors who are mostly experienced entrepreneurs and as such, understand what it is to be in your shoes. If the business fails, you are not obligated to return their money.

Don't let the term mislead you though. Angel Investors do **not** give free money; they are equity investors who will get a stake in your company as well as a say in the running of the business or at the minimum your accountability on business decisions – it is after all, their money! So, be prepared to let go of a portion of your future earnings (depending on whatever percentage of your company their investment yields) as well as a measure of control.

- **Venture Capitalists**: While somewhat similar to Angel Investors, Venture Capitalists focus on businesses that have enormous potential, especially in industries or trends that are more likely to generate significant return. Where Angel Investors are typically wealthy individuals who invest their own money, Venture Capitalists tend to be employees (of venture capital firms) overseeing professionally managed funds (i.e. of other people) which they invest. Unlike Angel Investors, VCs usually exit their stake in the business if it goes public (or is acquired), and tend to focus on businesses which have passed the startup phase, are already generating revenues and are looking to rapidly scale.
- **Business Incubators & Accelerators**: A good analogy for these terms would perhaps be the

difference between the ways a typical Mom or Dad relates with their child. Most mothers nurture their little ones, they coddle them and create quality time to cultivate and develop them. Quite a number of fathers on the other hand give their kids the more disciplined, 'tough' love that often demands them to take responsibility quickly☺. Consider Business Incubators to be Mothers and Accelerators, Fathers. Incubators are organizations dedicated to nurturing early stage businesses by providing coaching, office space and networking connections; you can gain invaluable expertise and mentorship, not to mention a variety of capital raising opportunities. Accelerators are similar but require (some would say demand!) you to grow more quickly and take that leap rather than small steps.

- **Competitions**: You may be surprised to discover that competitions have assisted in driving opportunities for fund raising. Through such contests, entrepreneurs with valid business ideas have platforms to showcase their product/pitch their business plan, pitting themselves against other entrepreneurs across similar or different industries. Asides the funding opportunity, there is also the added advantage of public exposure (via media coverage) which is quite beneficial for startups.

Getting investors of any kind to believe in your idea to the point of parting with their money means that your idea really must be worth funding...but I don't need to tell you that, do I ☺.

CHAPTER 7

THE PITCH: WRITING YOUR BUSINESS PLAN

"Going into business without a business plan is like going on a mountain trek without a map or GPS support – you'll eventually get lost and starve!''— Kevin J. Donaldson

Right, we've come to a critical moment: you have the purpose for your business, you've registered and structured it, you intend aligning with standards and you understand the numbers that will drive it.

But then you come to a turning point.

Some potential investors have indicated some interest in working with you but want to see your business plan. You've also gotten some additional partners who are keen on the idea but need to see a roadmap for the business. They need you, as the visionary, to supply the business plan so there is a guide, a compass that gives direction, helps the busines shoot straight and monitor the arrow's trajectory.

You know that you need a business plan to document the vision and for the business; something you can share with partners and potential investors, something to inspire the troops, something to show new recruits, something that indicates the business knows where it's going...

There's just one 'slight' problem: you don't know how to come up with one!

Relax...that's why we are here, together ☺

A Business plan is one of your most important – and strategic - tools, helping you achieve near, mid and long-term goals and keeping you focused on tracking the essential stages needed for the business to succeed. A good one will provide greater clarity (shine a brighter light☺) on all aspects of your business: marketing, finance, business operations and product/service specifics.

And let's not forget the oh-so-serious need for funding! Investors and Lenders need your business plan to determine if indeed you know what you're doing and if what you're doing is worth financing.

So yes...critical stuff. Simply put: no business plan = no business.

But before you get into the specifics of **how** to write your business plan, there are 2 things you need to ask yourself:

- Who is your Target Audience? Exactly who are the people that will be reading your plan? The best way to answer this is to first define the **objective** of the plan. If your goal is to raise capital (funding) then investors/lenders are your target audience. On the other hand, if you are seeking partnership with others or a joint venture, then your target audience would be potential business partners.
- What do you want their response to be? This means that depending on your target audience, the focus of your Business Plan should be the **key message** you want to pass. If the focus of the plan is to raise funds, then concentrating on how to jointly tackle the market would be the wrong message to pass and would not elicit the response you require (that is...if you get a response at all).

Traditional or Lean?

Once you've answered these questions, you're ready to begin writing the plan.

Because Business Plans communicate key sets of information to your audience, this means that rather than going through a very long process of thinking through what should go in there or not, we can use a format or template as a guide which helps us in focusing on the important sections of what constitutes a great business plan, and develop our material appropriately.

There are actually 2 types of Business Plan formats. At first glance, the difference between the two appears to be a case of old-school/new school. But I think it really goes beyond that. Let's look at each and consider them individually before we answer the question of suitability.

The Traditional Business Plan

By Traditional, this format focuses more on expectation. In other words when you write a traditional business plan, there are certain things your target audience **expects** you to talk about which if you don't, give the impression that you did a lazy job, are incompetent or don't really know your business well. Of course, none of these is an opinion you want your intended audience to form.

The key thing to note about the Traditional Business Plan is that it is extremely detailed and comprehensive. Naturally, it takes time to write and as such, requires you to be painstaking and thorough. Another key characteristic of this format is that this is typically the type of format prospective lenders and investors want to see when they ask for your business plan. So, if the goal of your plan is equity or debt financing, this is likely your go-to format.

What information should this format show?

Requirements

- **Executive Summary**: as the term implies, this is an overview of your business. What's the name of the business? What is its vision and mission? Outline what your company does and why you think your business will be successful. You could also include a mention about your product/service and organizational structure. Think of it as a documented version of your elevator pitch: if you were asked to give a concise but interesting summary of your business to a potential investor who could only give you 5 minutes, what would you say? That's your Executive Summary: key highlights that will get your audience interested. Think of it as a prelude to a first date: how you introduce and put yourself over determines if the other party deems you sufficiently interesting☺.
- **Company Profile/Description**: we need you to get more detailed about the company here. What problem(s) are you solving? Who are the potential customers, organizations, and businesses you plan to serve? This is a great place to talk about the strengths of your business; what makes it a beautiful bride? What is that 'something' you think makes your business stand out; your USP/UVP (unique selling/value point/proposition)? In thinking through and creating this, you could try adopting this formula: UVP/USP = Result Customer Wants + Specific Period of Time + Address

Objections. E.g. "Quality food delivered to your door in 30 minutes or it's free". This clearly tells the customer he will get what he wants within a specific time and the benefit that he gains if the business fails to deliver on its promise. This will force you to focus on the customer instead of your product.

- **Product/Service**: Let's have an in-depth description of your offering(s) here. In other words what is your product/service all about? How does it benefit customers? Does your product have a life cycle? If it does, explain it. You could try getting creative in this section, by adding some pictorial content to arrest the eye and make the presentation visually appealing.
- **Market Analysis**: Naturally before you launch out, you need to have done quite a bit of deep research of your intended market. The results of that go here and includes competitor analysis (a review of other companies offering similar product/services), and their strengths. Which are those that are successful? What did they do and why do you think it works? Most importantly, why do you think YOU can do it better?
- **Marketing Strategy**: this answers the question of how you plan on getting customers through the door. It's one thing to start a business, but if you have no definite plan of how you want to attract and retain customers, how can you expect

investors (or partners) to align with you? This section should give a thorough description of your sales and marketing strategy. Walk us through how an actual sale happens. What are your organic (offline) distribution channels? How do you plan on keeping your customers invested and what ways are you planning on scaling the business to ensure this? Customer attraction and retention are the crux of the business and your audience will be on the look out to see if you've done your homework...properly.

- **Organization and Management**: we've discussed structuring the business; this is what goes here. Let's see the organizational hierarchy and tell us what the business structure is. If you are fortunate to have some well-known names on your board, flaunt them.
- **Funding Request**: if the focus of your plan is to seek funding, this will be the key message. State and outline your request: how much do you need and over what period? What do you intend using the requested funds for (asset creation, cash flow, bills payments)? It is important to include your future strategic financial plans (e.g. paying off debt or selling part of the business) and critical for you to mention if you seek **Equity** or **Debt** financing. Either option will have an impact on your financials, so you really need to have thought this through.

- **Financial Projections**: the key to structuring the funding request is in realizing that the object is to convince the investor/lender to give you funds. Realizing that investors/lenders are also human beings who require a healthy ROI (Return on Investment) will enable you include all information that depicts your business will be stable and successful. The most critical of this is of course, your financials. Normally, financiers will want to see your historical (past) results as well as your forecast for the future. However for startups, historical financials will be replaced by your outlook and forecast for the business which, as we've discussed in understanding the numbers, are your sales forecasts, income projections and breakeven analysis (in addition to your Balance Sheet, Income Statement and Cash Flow).

Quite a bit isn't it? ☺

The Lean Startup Business Plan

The Lean Startup format is more high level and contains only key elements. Why is it called Lean Startup? Because compared to the elaborate planning required to produce the traditional business plan, this focuses more on experimentation and enables you explain what your business is about quickly, getting right to the point. The 'new school' vibe of this format is more popular with businesses which have relatively simple business concepts - especially for those with plans that are bound to be adapted or refined as they progress.

Obviously, it's quicker to write and not as detailed as the traditional plan. You simply state salient points about the business proposition, infrastructure, customers, and finances, and outline the fundamental facts. In developing this format, it's a good idea to think through the following, which will enable you think address each section holistically.

Requirements

- **Value Proposition**: Clearly describe the unique value you deliver to the customer. Which one of your customer's problems are you helping to solve? What products and services are you offering?
- **Partners**: Who are the other businesses or services you'll work with to run your business (especially useful if you are engaging in B2B)? The information should include key partners, suppliers, and resources.
- **Key Activities**: What key activities do your value propositions need? What distribution channels will you use? What will your customer relationships look like? What are your revenue streams? Here, focus on what way your operations/activities will be unique in the market.

- **Key Resources**: What are the assets required for your value propositions to be actualized (including staff and capital)?
- **Customer Segments**: Who are you creating value for? Who would you say are your most important customers?
- **Customer Relationships**: What type of relationship do you need to create and maintain with your customer segments. Will it be automated? Offline? What is the A-Z of the customer experience?
- **Channels**: How will you get in touch with your customer segments? Do you intend having a cohesive channels structure? How will they integrate? Which ones are more effective and cost-efficient? How will you incorporate them into customer procedures?
- **Cost**: Once you understand your infrastructure, what are the most important costs integral to your business model? Which key resources and activities are most expensive? Will you focus on cost reduction or maximizing value?
- **Revenue**: How will you make money? Are you dependent on single or multiple streams of income? If multiple, how much will each stream contribute to your total earnings? How much are your customers are willing to pay? How will they pay, and what will be their preferred mode of payment?

Which format will work better for you? Each format has distinct advantages, but the determining factor will be context; and context is everything, as they say.

What do I mean? Well, say you really believe the lean startup format will better work for you but your potential lender or investor wants to have more information. They want figures and graphs, they want to see your product lifecycle, they want to be absolutely sure before they hand over money.

Or if you've written the most beautiful, elegant business plan that ever was but all you hear is: 'can you just give me the essentials?'

What do you do then? Tell them that your lean startup/traditional business plan is *really* the way to go and if they're not comfortable with it, they can take a hike?

I thought not☺.

If you ask me, I don't think there's any harm in learning both formats and utilizing each as they benefit you.

Learn.

The Pitch Deck

But let's consider another scenario.

How about if you find yourself in the rueful (but all too regular) position of having no potential investors knocking on the door to ask for your business plan? Do you sit around waiting, praying that the sun shines brighter tomorrow?

No, you do not. You get creative. You get proactive. You get a Pitch deck.

What is a Pitch Deck? The best way to describe it would be the story of your business – in visuals.

It is essentially a visual summary of your business that you can send to potential investors as a means of piquing their interest. While not necessarily meant to be presented, you absolutely should use it if asked to present or if you get selected for a pitch competition.

The main objective of a Pitch Deck is to generate sufficient attention from your audience which will lead to a deeper conversation. Simply put, it helps an investor see your current position (where you are) and your intended goal (where you want to be); based on this information, they can then decide if they want to join you in the journey.

From the earlier part of this chapter, you know that a business plan (particularly the traditional variant) takes a lot of effort to produce and a while to read through and digest. As such, you don't want to use this immediately, when you are seeking attention. A pitch deck allows you to give the basic and pertinent information an investor needs to make up his mind if to pursue a serious funding conversation with you; therefore, it's wiser to only send a business plan when you are explicitly asked to provide one - this is a clear sign that the other party is ready to discuss business.

You can infer from the above that the Pitch Deck is not, nor should it be, a replacement for a proper Business Plan. In some cases, it is not even necessary. For instance, in Debt Financing via the local bank say, you should not proffer a pitch deck to the prospective lender. What the bank wishes to see is good, sound business plan that they can use to make a lending decision. Pitch Decks tend to work better in an Equity Financing situation where the Investor will ultimately be a shareholder in the business.

One more thing: please realize that because the essence of the pitch deck is visuals, you need to be pretty adept with infographics or get the services of someone who is. No one will be interested in a hastily put together PowerPoint slides with a lot of text and a few circles and squares ☺.

P.S.

"Good business leaders create a vision, articulate the vision, passionately own the vision, and relentlessly drive it to completion." - Jack Welch

Yay, you're done!

Well, no actually. You're just beginning...

I said at the start that you're going to need Light. It is my hope and prayer that this book has been able to shine some light in you and provide you with knowledge that you need.

This is not an easy road you've chosen; there will be dark days and dark nights; there will be moments of doubt and despair; there will be days when all you want to do is throw in the towel.

You're going to have to pour out your heart to make this happen.

But the edge that Winners have over others is their refusal to bow down before circumstances: their Faith in the face of Despair; their Courage in the face of fear; their Light in the face of darkness.

It is the quality of your heart; the light in your mind that will transform you and make you accomplish great things.

So...

Believe in your heart...

Focus in your mind...

Declare it with your mouth...

Work at it every day...

And it will come to pass.

Godspeed,

W.

APPENDICES

Free Financial Statement and Business Plan Templates

Appendix 1 – Lean Startup Business Plan Template

XYZ Company	
Value Proposition	Key Relationships
Partners	Key Activities
Competition	Revenue streams
Marketing activities	Cost Structure
Team and key roles	Target Market

Appendix 2: Income Statement Template

Income Statement Template

	$	$
Sales (Revenue)		
Income		
Expenses		
*****		
*****		
*****		
*****		
*****		
*****		
*****		
Depreciation		
*****		
*****		
Total	0	0
Net Income		0

Appendix 3: Balance Sheet Template

Balance Sheet Template

Assets ($)

Current Assets
Cash
*****
*****

Long-term Assets
Asset item at cost
Less: Accumulated Depreciation   0
Asset item at cost
Less: Accumulated Depreciation   ______   ______ 0   ______ 0

Total Assets   **0**

Liabilities ($)

Current Liabilities
Long Term Liabilities
Payable to Consultant   ______

Total Liabilities   0

Owner's Equity ($)

Original Investment
Retained Earnings**   ______

Total owner's equity   ______ 0

Total liabilities and owner's equity   **0**

** for subsequent period based on first period Income Statement

Appendix 4: Basic Cash Flow Template

Cash Flow - Basic Template

Outflows	$
*****	
*****	
*****	
*****	
*****	
*****	
*****	
*****	
*****	
Total	-
Inflows	
*****	
*****	
*****	
Total	-
Net Cash Inflow	-

Appendix 5: Cash Flow by Activity Template

Statement of Cash Flow By Activity Template

	$	$
Cash Flow : Operating Activities		
Inflow from Sales		
Outflows		
*****		
*****		
*****		
*****		
*****		
*****		0
Net Cash from Operations		**0**
Cash Flow : Investing Activities		
Inflows		
*****		
*****		
Outflows		
****		
****		
Net Cash from Investments		**0**
Cash Flow : Financing Activities		
Inflows		
****		
****		
Outflows		
****		
****		
Loan Repayment (principal)		
Net Cash from Financing		**0**
Net Cash Inflow		-